Piano ✹ Vocal ✹ Guitar

SUMMER OF 1969

40 Songs of Peace & Love
That Were Played at Woodstock

ISBN 978-1-4234-8075-4

CORPORATION
7777 W. BLUEMOUND RD. P.O. BOX 13819 MILWAUKEE, WI 53213

Visit Hal Leonard Online at
www.halleonard.com

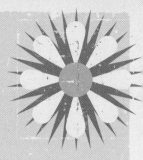

ACID QUEEN

Words and Music by
PETE TOWNSHEND

Fairly bright

If your child ain't all he

should be now, _____ this girl {could/will} put him right. I'll

show him what he could be now, just give me one _____

night. I'm the gyp - sy, the

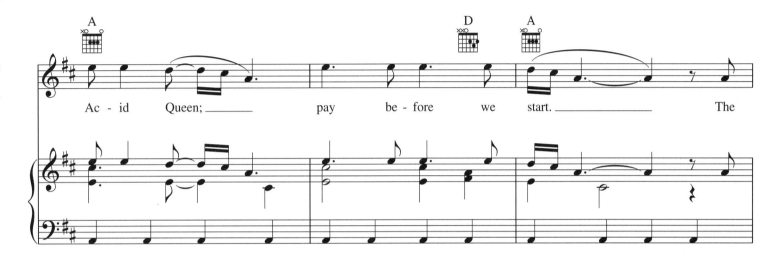

Ac - id Queen; _____ pay be - fore we start. _____ The

gyp - sy, I'm guar - an - teed ___ to tear your soul a -

part. Give us a room ___ and close the door;

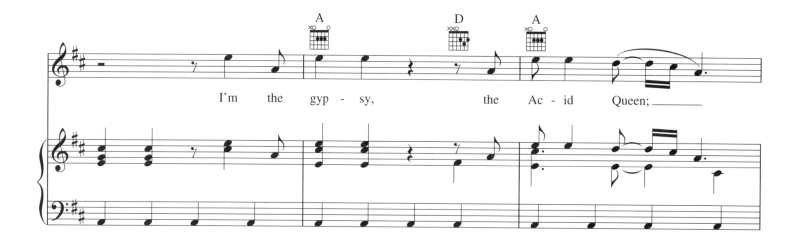

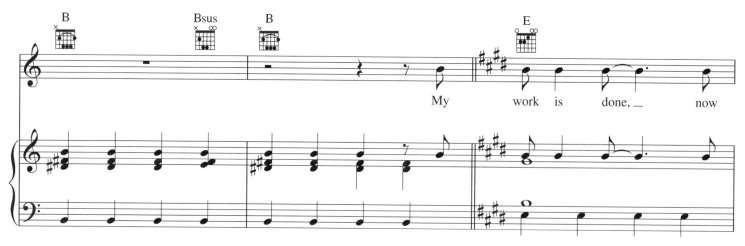

My work is done, __ now

look at him, he's nev-er been more __ a - live. His

head, it shakes, __ his fin-gers clutch, __ watch his bod-y ____

writhe. I'm ____ the gyp-sy, the

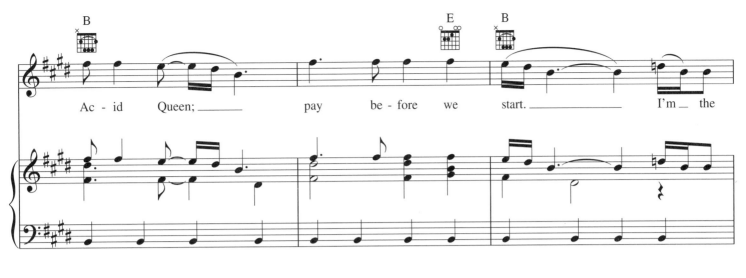

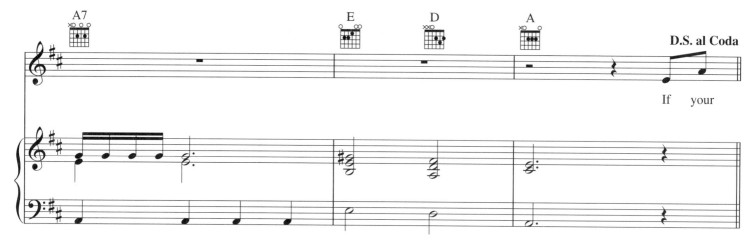

D.S. al Coda

If your

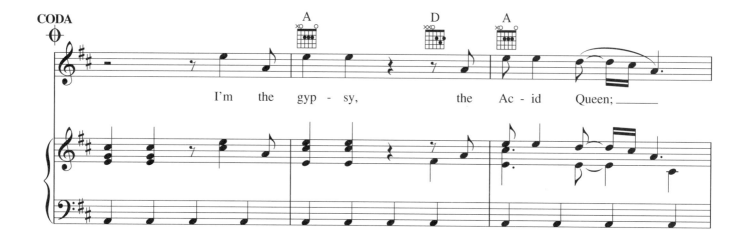

CODA

I'm the gyp - sy, the Ac - id Queen; _____

pay be - fore we start. _____ The gyp - sy, I'm

guar - an - teed ___ to tear your soul a - part.

BALL AND CHAIN

Words and Music by
WILLIE MAE (BIG MAMA) THORNTON

In a slow 2

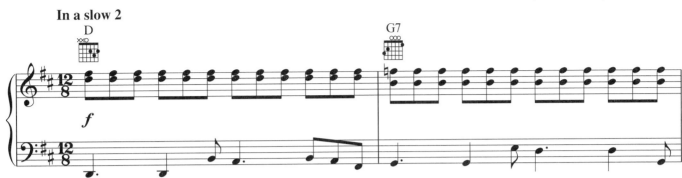

(1.) Sit - tin' by my win - dow, and I was look - in' out
(2.,4.) oh, oh, ba - by, why you wan - na do these
(3.) *(Spoken:) I know you gonna miss me, baby, oh yes, you're gonna miss*

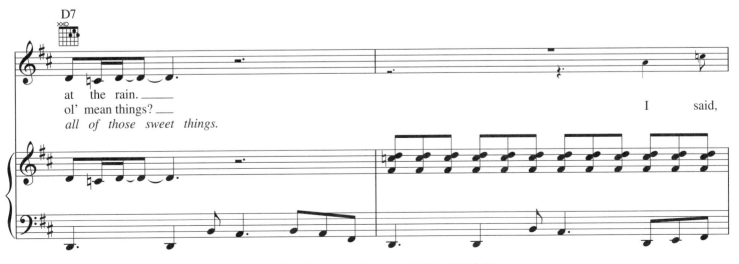

at the rain. I said,
ol' mean things?
all of those sweet things.

Sit - tin' by my win - dow, ba - by, and __ I was sit - tin' there
oh, oh, _____ ba - by, why __ you wan - na do these __
I know you're gonna miss me, baby, *you're gonna miss all of those*

_____ look - in' out ____ at the rain. _
_____ ol' mean things ____ to me? _
sweet, sweet things. *And then you'll find*

You know ____ some-thin' struck me, clamped on to me just
Be - cause __ you know I love you, and I'm so sick and
that your whole life will be like mine, *all wrapped up*

BEAUTIFUL PEOPLE

Words and Music by
MELANIE SAFKA

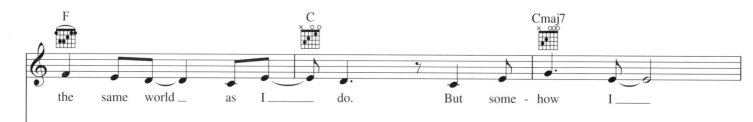

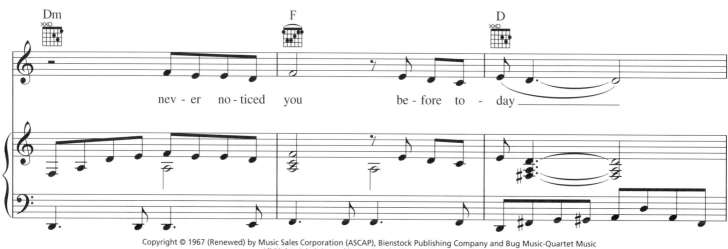

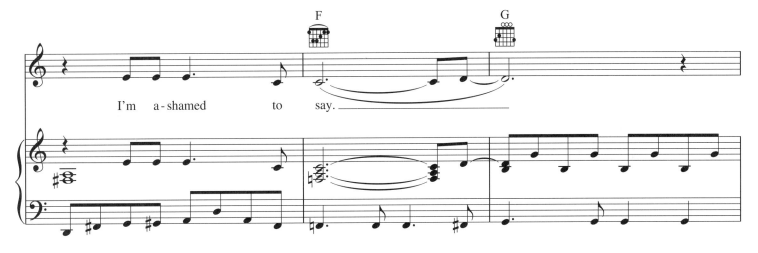

I'm a-shamed to say. _____

Beau - ti - ful peo - ple, we ___ share the ___

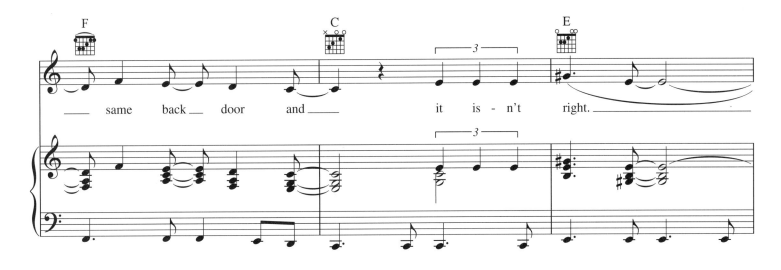

___ same back ___ door and ___ it is - n't right. _____

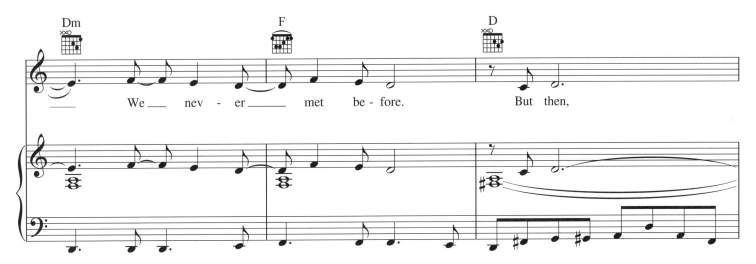

___ We ___ nev - er _____ met be - fore. But then,

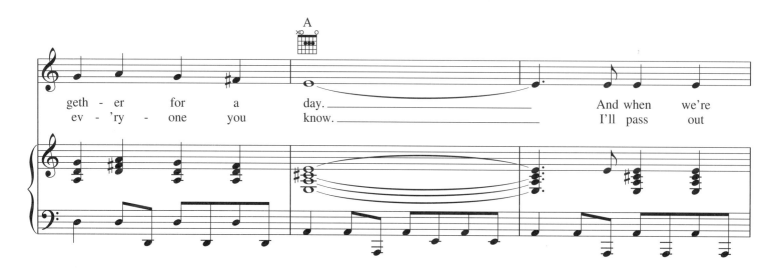

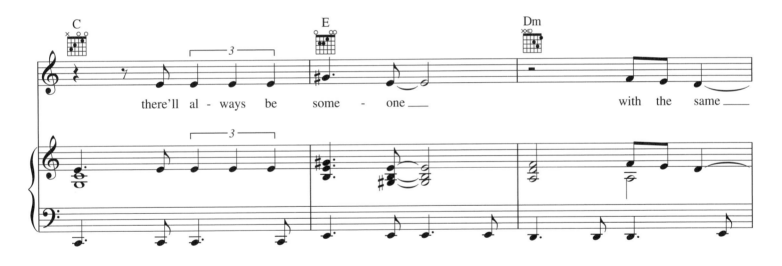

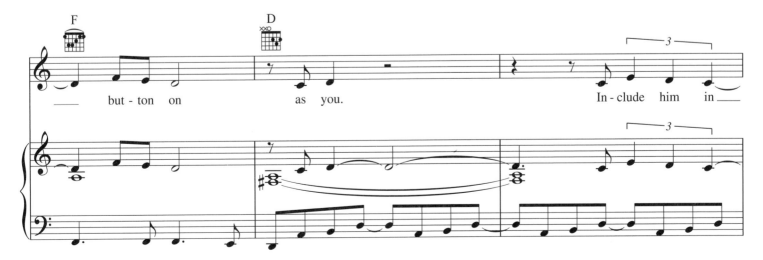

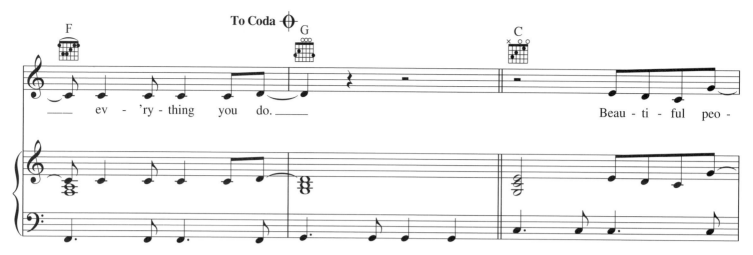

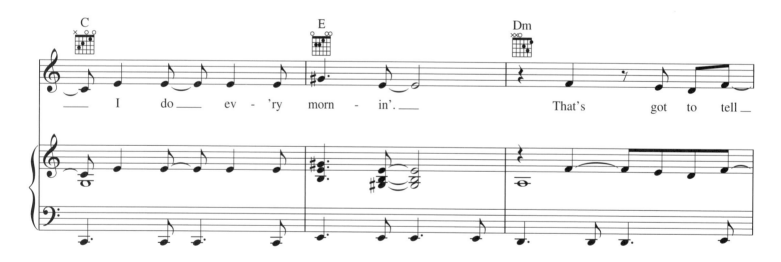

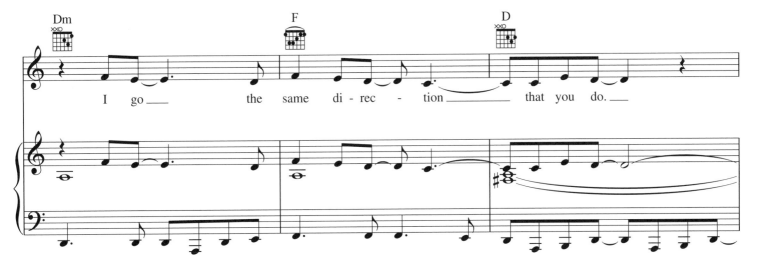

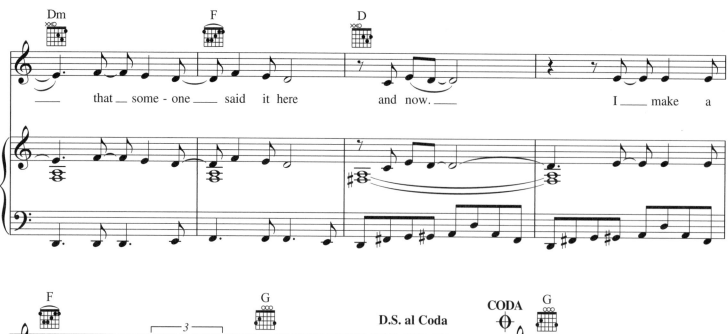

that __ some-one __ said it here and now. __ I __ make a

vow __ that some-time, some - how

D.S. al Coda

CODA

He may be

sit - ting right next to you.

Repeat and Fade

He may be a beautiful people, too.
And if you take care of him,

Optional Ending

maybe he'll take care of you.

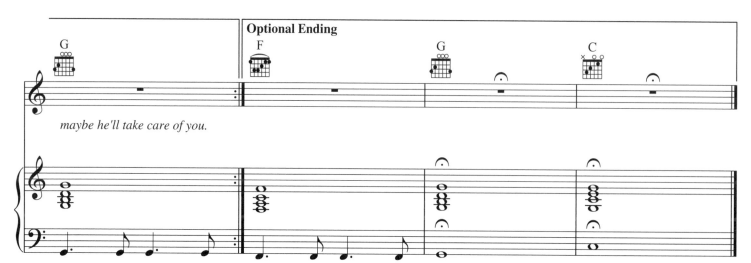

GOOD MORNING
LITTLE SCHOOLGIRL

Words and Music by
WILLIE WILLIAMSON

Good morn - in', lit - tle school - girl.
know what,
air - plane.

Good morn - in', lit - tle school - girl.
some - times __ I don't know what,
I'm gon - na buy me an air - plane.

Can I __ come
what in the world, __
Fly __ right

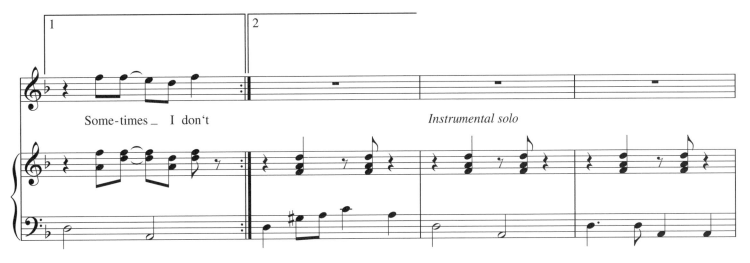

BORN UNDER A BAD SIGN

Words and Music by BOOKER T. JONES
and WILLIAM BELL

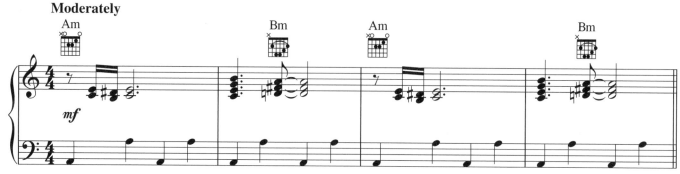

When I was just a little boy, my daddy left home. He

left me and my mama to go it all alone. You know, the times were hard, but somehow we survived.

Lord knows, it's a mystery to me how she managed to keep us alive.

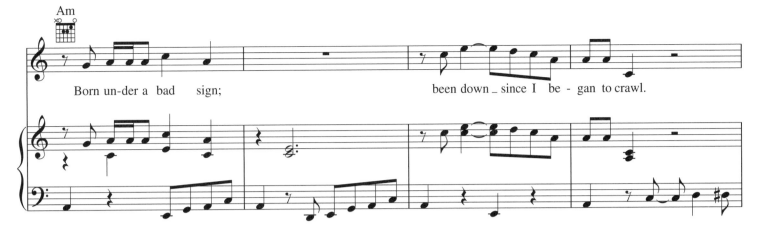

Born un-der a bad sign; been down _ since I be - gan to crawl.

Oh, if it was-n't for bad ___ luck, _ I would-n't have no luck at all. (Let ___ me tell you.)

Hard luck and trou - ble
I can't read; I nev - er
Wine and wom - en is

is my on - ly friend; Been on my own ev - er since I was ten.
learned how to write. My whole life has been one big fight.
all I _____ crave; A big head wom-an will ___ car-ry me to my grave.

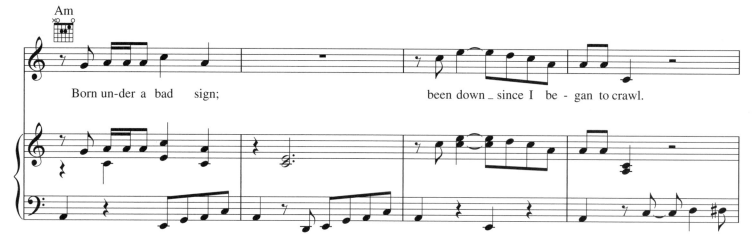

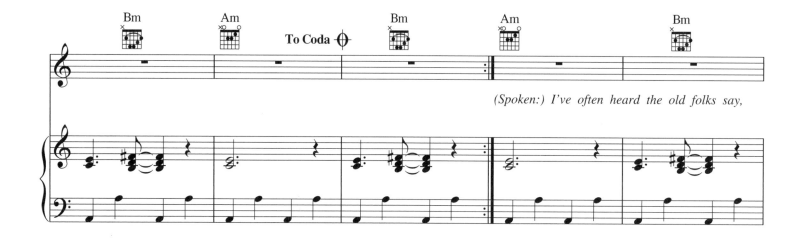

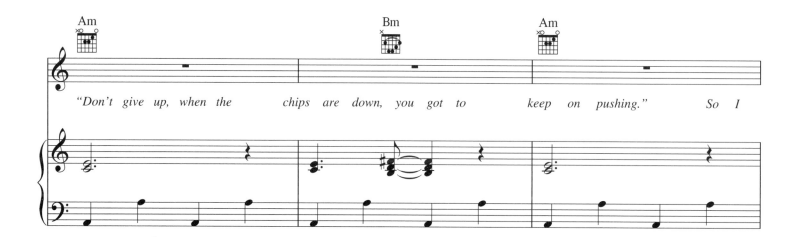

guess I gotta keep on pushing. You see, I was down, but I

kind of picked myself up a little bit, oh, and I had to dust myself off,

clean myself up, and now, I'm gonna keep on pushing; I can't stop.

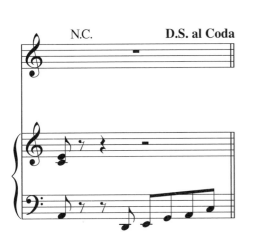

(Spoken ad lib.)
I'm gonna get myself together now,
I'm gonna keep on pushing.

DRUG STORE TRUCK DRIVIN' MAN

Words and Music by ROGER McGUINN
and GRAM PARSONS

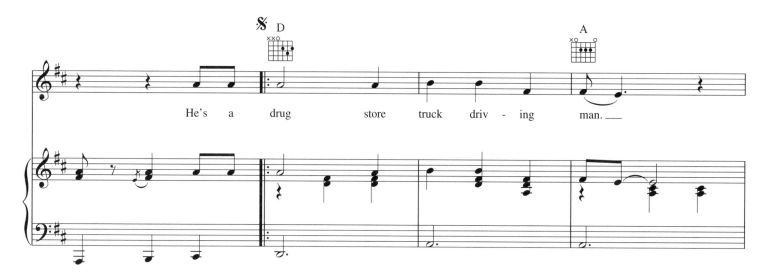

He's a drug store truck driv-ing man. ____

He's the head of ____ the Ku Klux Klan. ____

When sum - mer _____ rolls a - round,

To Coda

he'll be luck - y if he's not in town. _____

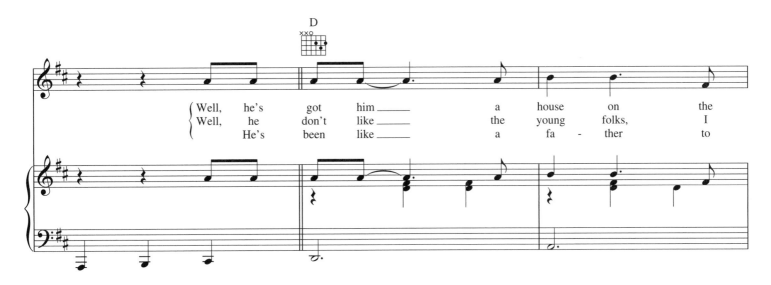

Well, he's got him _____ a house on the
Well, he don't like _____ the young folks, I
He's been like _____ a fa - ther to

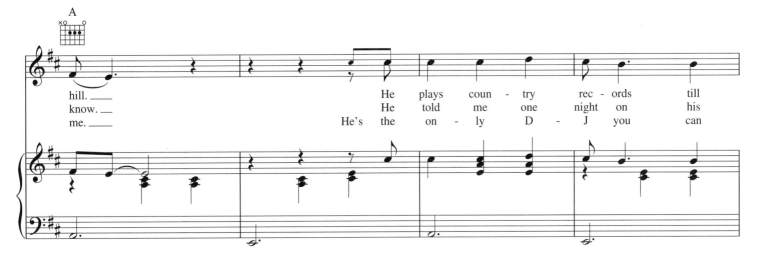

hill. _____ He plays coun - try rec - ords till
know. _____ He told me one night on his
me. _____ He's the on - ly D - J you can

you've had your fill._____ He's a
ra - di - o show._____ He's
hear af - ter three._____ I'm an

fire - man's friend; he's an all - night D. J._____
got him a med - al he won in the war._____
all - night mu - si - cian in a rock - and - roll band,_____

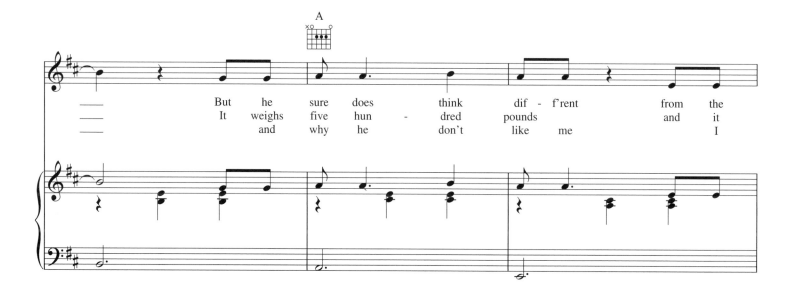

_____ But he sure does think dif - f'rent from the
_____ It weighs five hun - dred pounds and it
_____ and why he don't like me I

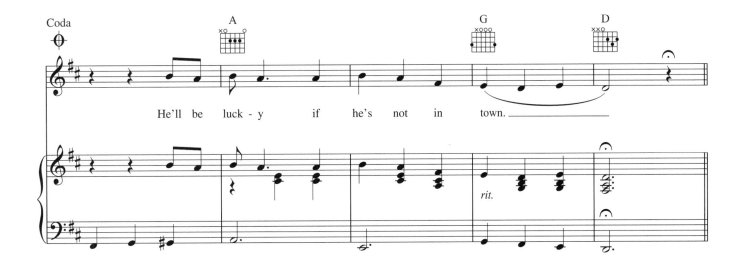

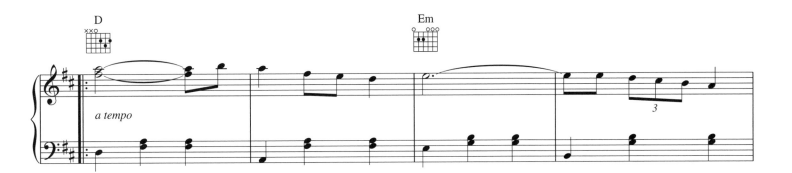

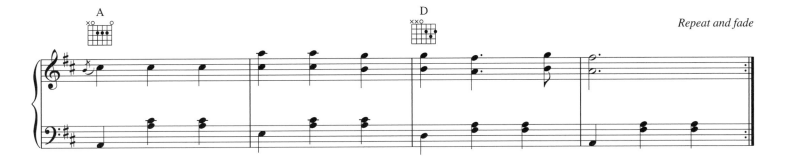

FOR YASGUR'S FARM

Words and Music by GAIL COLLINS,
GEORGE GARDOS, CORKY LAING,
FELIX PAPPALARDI, DAVID REA
and GARY SHIP

Moderate Rock

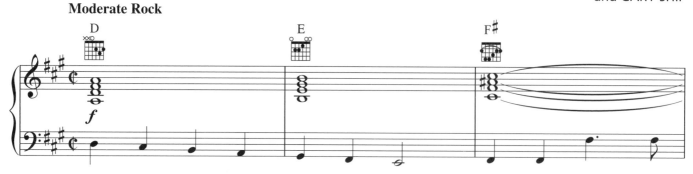

Who am I but you and the sun?

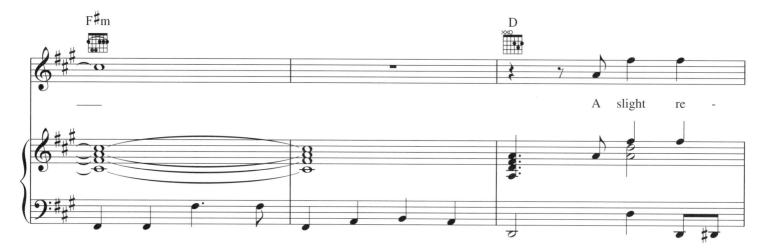

A slight re-

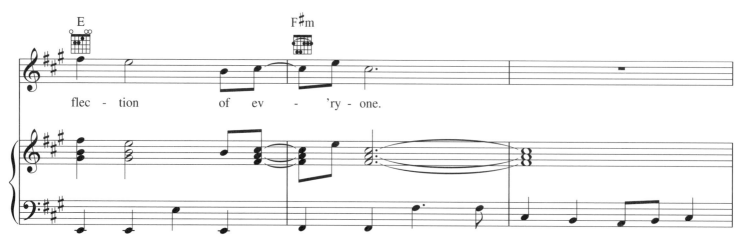

flec - tion of ev - 'ry - one.

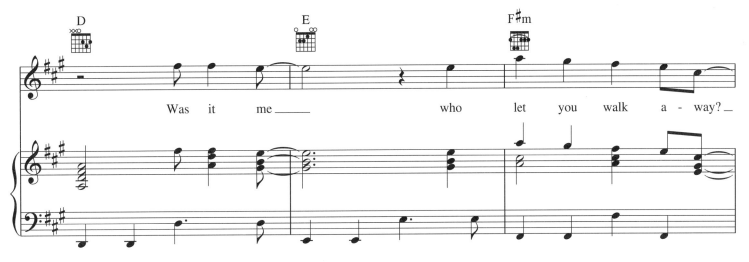

Was it me _____ who let you walk a - way?___

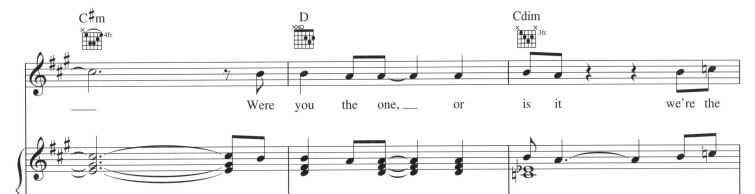

____ Were you the one, ___ or is it we're the

same? _____

What are we in
Love is on - ly
Instrumental solo

time go - in' by? _____
what we come to live. _____

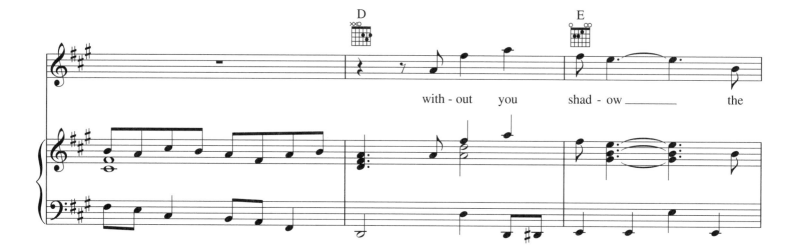

you the one, ___ or is it we're the same? _____

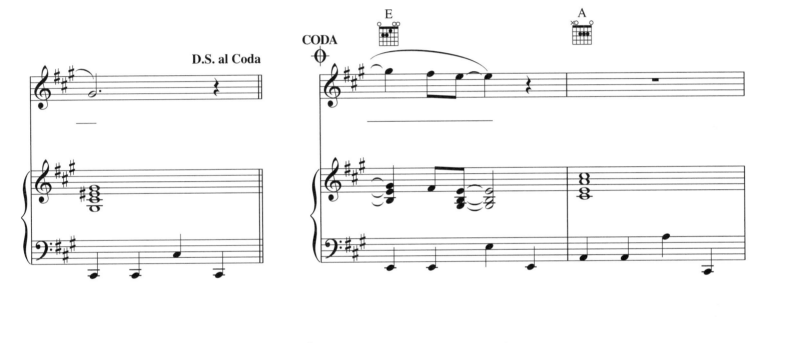

D.S. al Coda   CODA

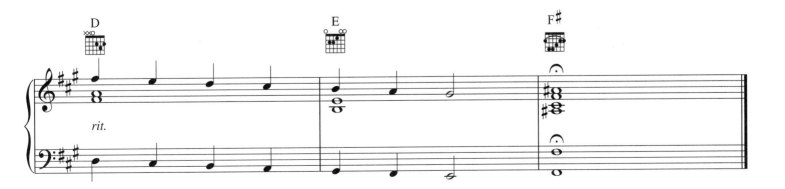

rit.

HELPLESSLY HOPING

Words and Music by
STEPHEN STILLS

Moderately fast

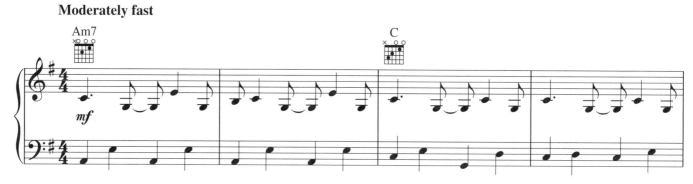

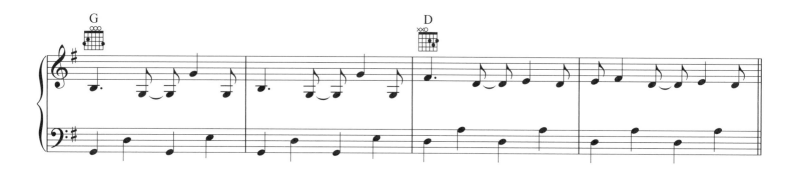

Help - less - ly hop - ing, __ her har - le - quin hov - ers __ near -

by, a - wait - ing __ a word. __

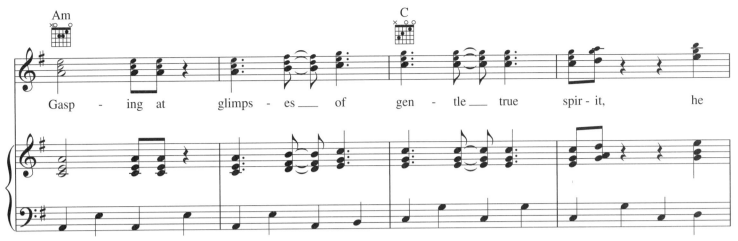

Am   C

Gasp - ing at glimps - es ___ of gen - tle ___ true spir - it, he

G   D

runs,   wish-ing he ___ could fly, _____ on - ly to

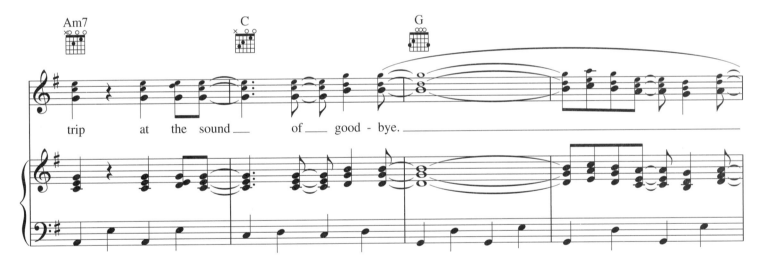

Am7   C   G

trip   at the sound ___ of ___ good - bye. _____

D   Am

___   Word - less - ly watch - ing, ___ he
           Stand by the stair - way, ___ you'll

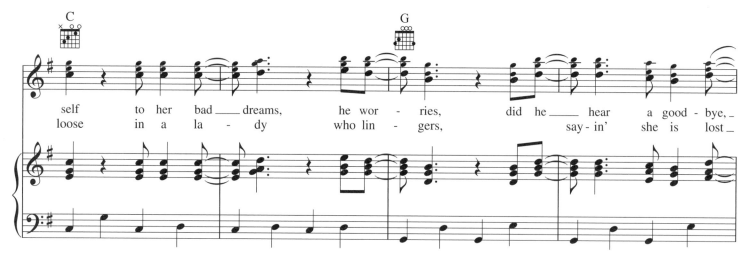

They are one _____ per - son, they are two__

____ a - lone, _____ they are three _____ to - geth -

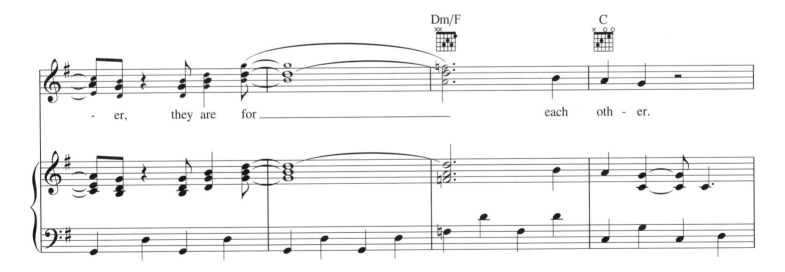

- er, they are for _____ each oth - er.

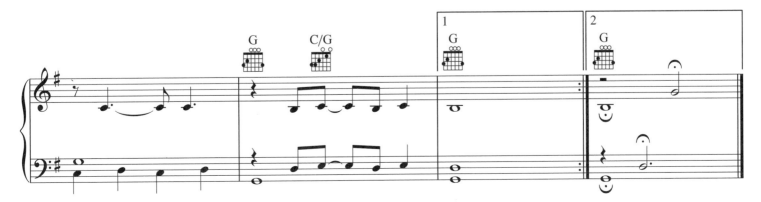

HEY JOE

Words and Music by
BILLY ROBERTS

Moderately slow Rock

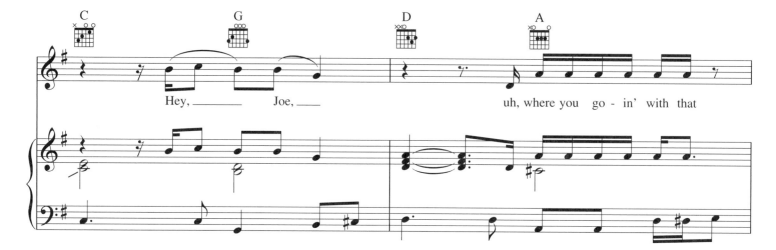

Hey, _____ Joe, _____ uh, where you go - in' with that

gun in your hand?

Hey, _____ Joe, I said where you goin' with that gun

in your hand? _ Al - right.

I'm go - in' down to shoot my old la - dy, you know I caught her mess-in' 'round with an - oth -

er man. Yeah.

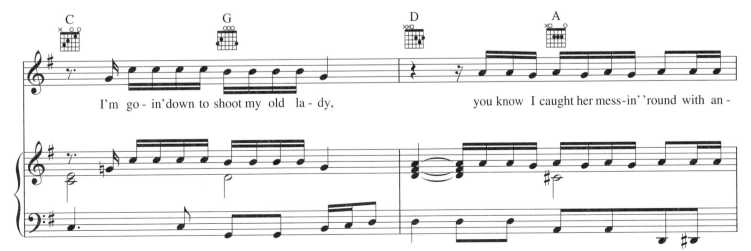

I'm go - in' down to shoot my old la - dy, you know I caught her mess-in' 'round with an -

oth - er man. Huh! And that ain't too cool.

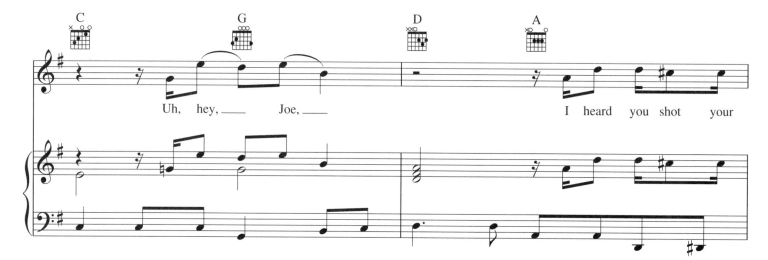

Uh, hey, ___ Joe, ___ I heard you shot your

wom-an down, _ you shot her down now. ___

Uh, hey, ___ Joe, I heard you shot your old

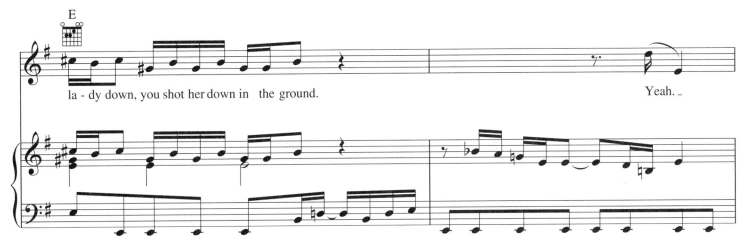

la - dy down, you shot her down in the ground.   Yeah. __

Yes, I ___ did, I shot her.   You know I caught her mess - in' 'round,

mess - in' 'round town. __

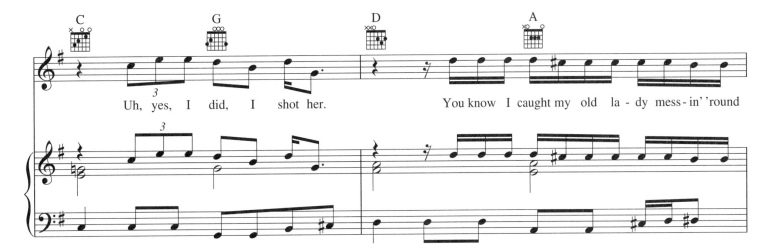

Uh, yes, I did, I shot her.   You know I caught my old la - dy mess - in' 'round

town. _____ And I gave her the gun. I shot her.

Al - right. _

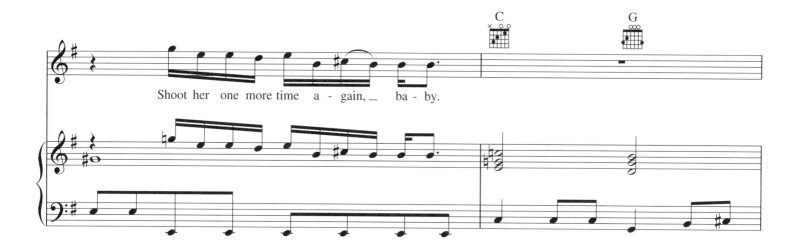

Shoot her one more time a - gain, _ ba - by.

Yeah.

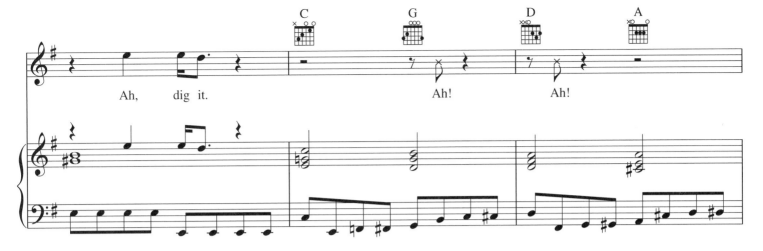

Ah, dig it. Ah! Ah!

Al - right.

Hey, _____ Joe, said now, uh, where you gon - na run

to now? _____ Where you gon - na run to? _____ Yeah.

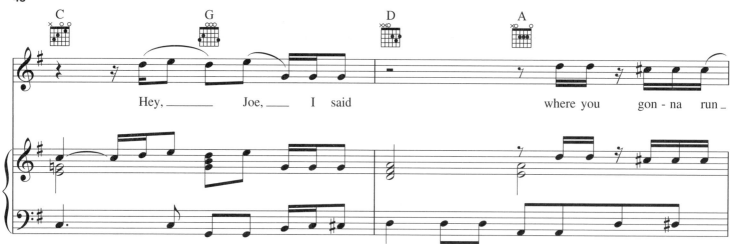

Hey, _____ Joe, _____ I said _____ where you gon-na run _____

_____ to now? _____ Where you, where you gon-na go? _____ Well, dig it.

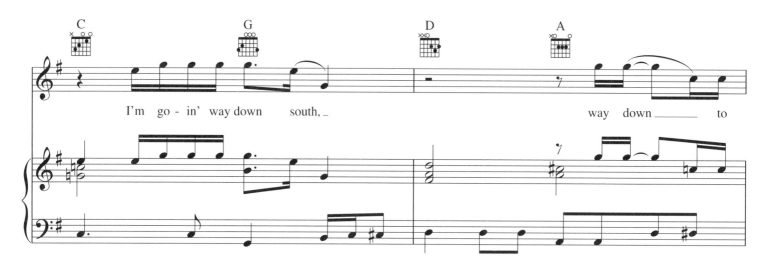

I'm go-in' way down south, _____ way down _____ to

Mex-i-co _____ way. _____ Al - right. _____

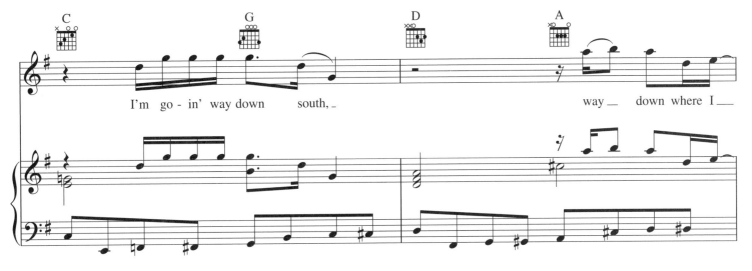

I'm go-in' way down south, __ way __ down where I __

__ can be free. Ain't no one __ gon-na find me, babe.

Ain't no hang-man gon-na, he ain't gon-na put a rope a-round

Repeat ad lib. and Fade

me. You bet-ter be-lieve __ it right __ now. __ I got-ta go __ now.

HIGH FLYING BIRD

Words and Music by
BILLY WHEELER

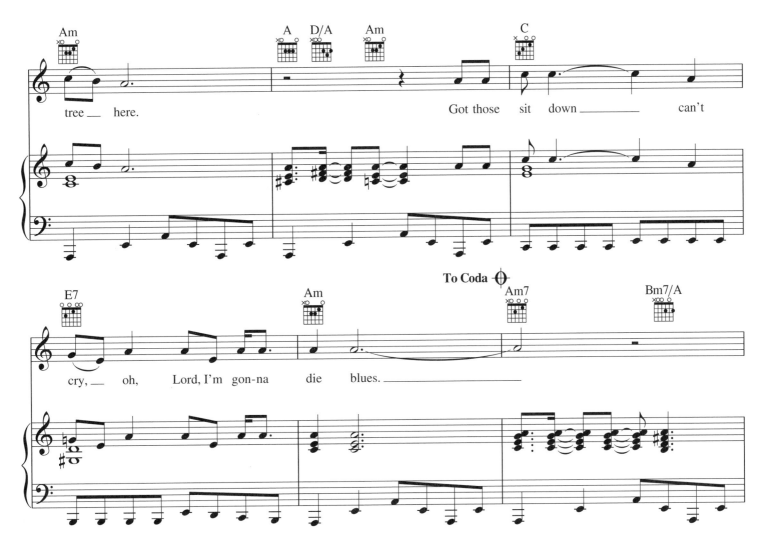

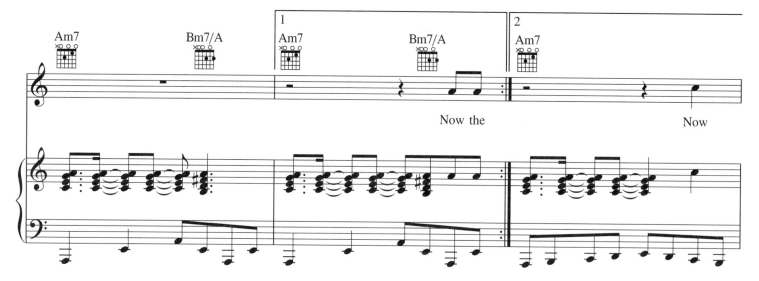

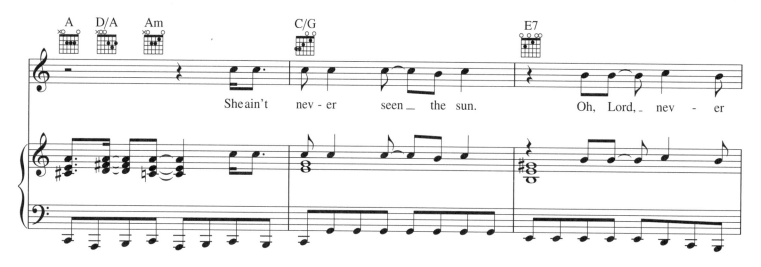

woman ____ up and died. Lord, ____ she up and

died now. ____ Oh, Lord, ____ she up and died ____ now. ____

And she want - ed to fly ____ and the on - ly way to fly ____ is

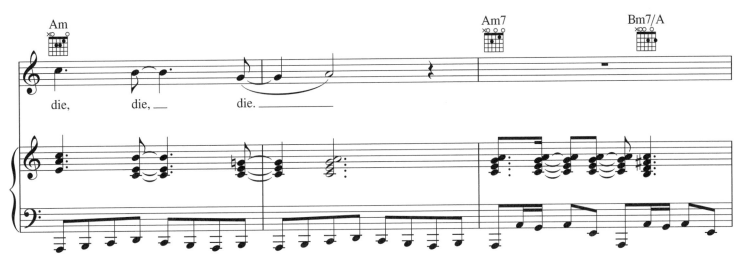

die, die, ____ die. ____

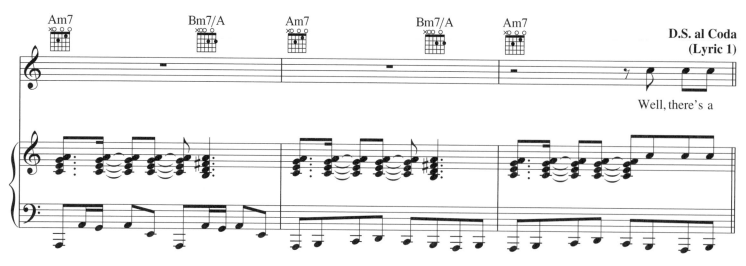

HOW HAVE YOU BEEN

Words and Music by
JOHN SEBASTIAN

Lyrics:

How have you been, my dar-ling chil-dren, _____ while I have been a-way in the west? _____ Though you are stran-gers, I

56

feel that I know __ you _____ by the way that you

treat __ me __ and of - fer __ to feed me __ and ea - ger - ly

ask ____ if I'll stay for a rest. __

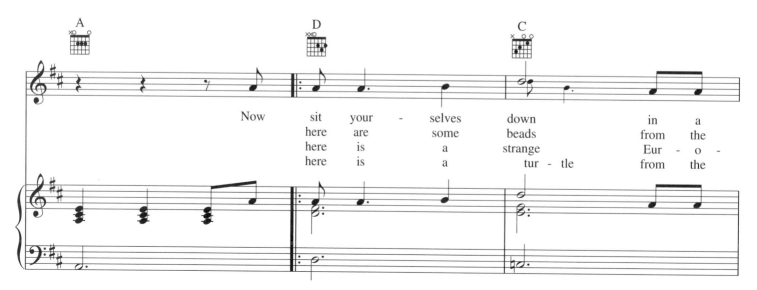

Now sit your - selves down in a
here are some beads in from the
here is a strange Eur - o -
here is a tur - tle from the

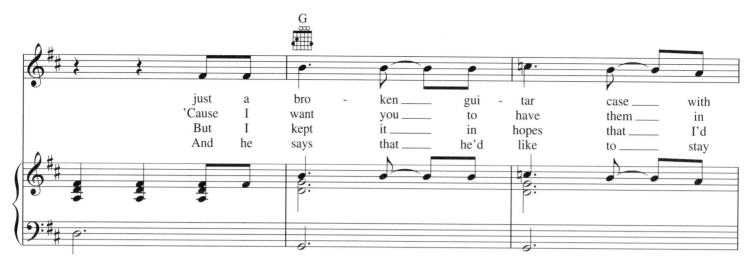

just a bro- ken _____ gui- tar case _____ with
'Cause I I want you _____ to have them _____ in
But I I kept it _____ in hopes that _____ I'd
And he says that _____ he'd like to _____ stay

tape _____ on _____ the sides, a bag _____ and a
hopes _____ that _____ you'll be as love- ly _____ as the
use _____ it _____ some- day. It's fun- ny _____ how _____
here _____ in _____ your yard. At long last _____ his _____

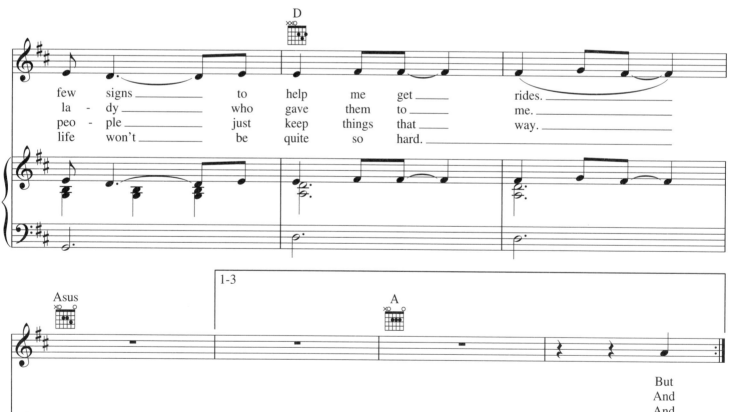

few signs _____ to help me get _____ rides. _____
la - dy _____ who gave them to _____ me. _____
peo- ple _____ just keep things that _____ way. _____
life won't _____ be quite so hard. _____

1-3

Asus   A

But
And
And

treat _____ me _____ and of - fer _____ to feed me _____ and

eag - er - ly ask _____ if I'll stay for a

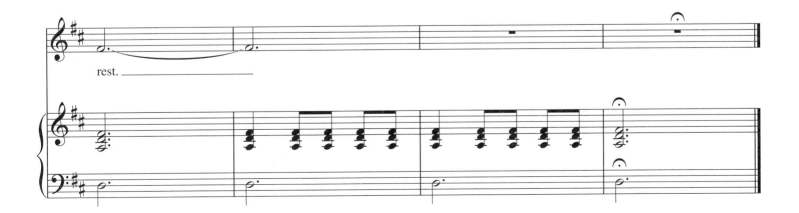

rest. _____

I CAN'T EXPLAIN

Words and Music by
PETER TOWNSHEND

Bright Rock

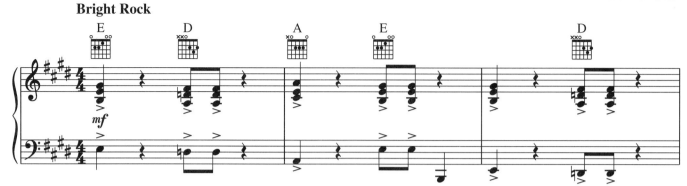

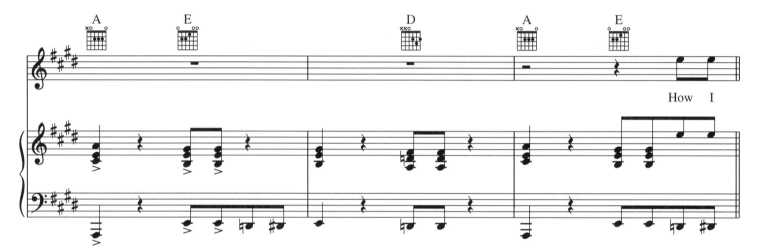

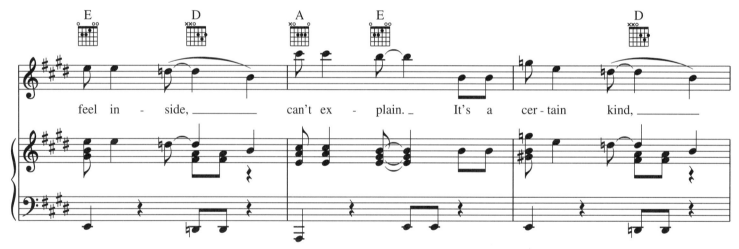

down in my soul, yeah can't ex - plain. _ I said

can't ex - plain. _ I'm feel - in' good now, yeah, but can't ex - plain. _

Diz - zy in the head _ and I'm _ feel - in' blue. _ The things you say, well, may -
Diz - zy in the head _ and I'm _ feel - in' bad. _ The things you said _ got _

- be they're true. }   I'm get - tin' fun - ny dreams a - gain _ and a - gain. _ I
_ me real mad. }

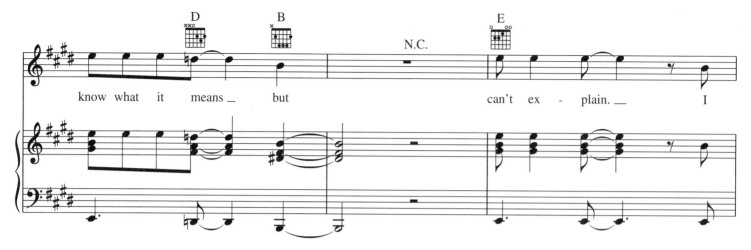

D.S. al Coda

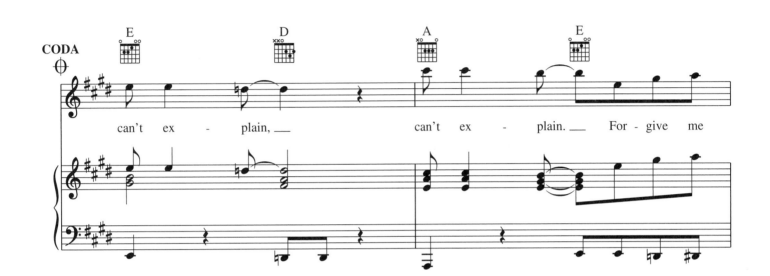

can't ex - plain, ____ can't ex - plain. ____ For - give me

one more time __ now, can't ex - plain. _

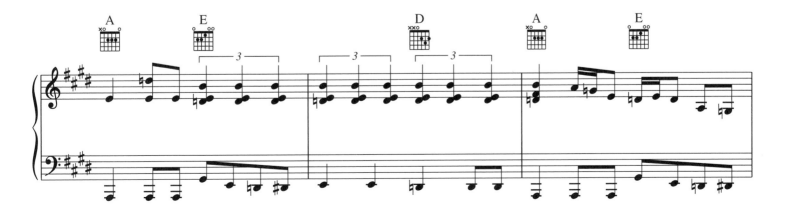

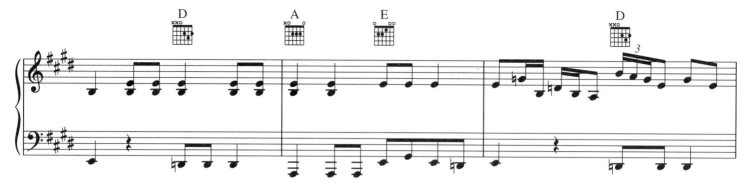

Said I can't ex - plain __ it.

You drive me out of my mind. Yeah, I'm the

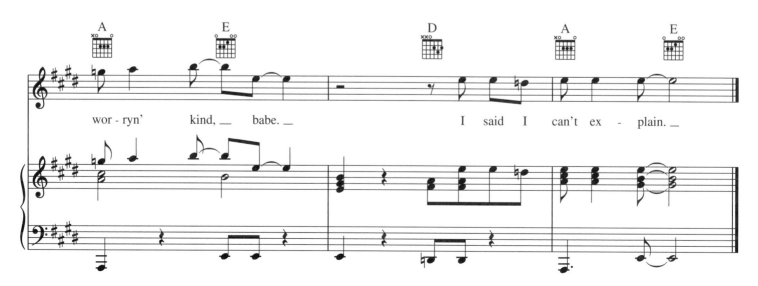

wor - ryn' kind, __ babe. __ I said I can't ex - plain. __

I SHALL BE RELEASED

Words and Music by
BOB DYLAN

1. They say ___ ev - 'ry man must need pro - tec - tion, ___
2., 3. (See additional lyrics)

they say ev - 'ry man ___ must

fall. ___

Yet I swear ___ I see ___ my re -

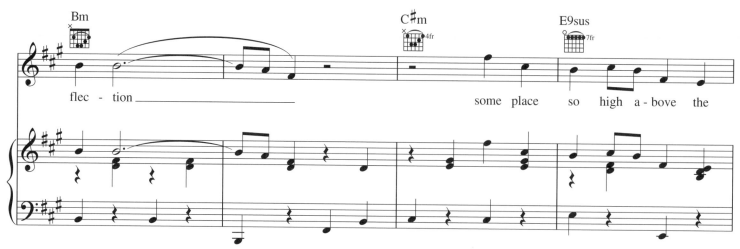

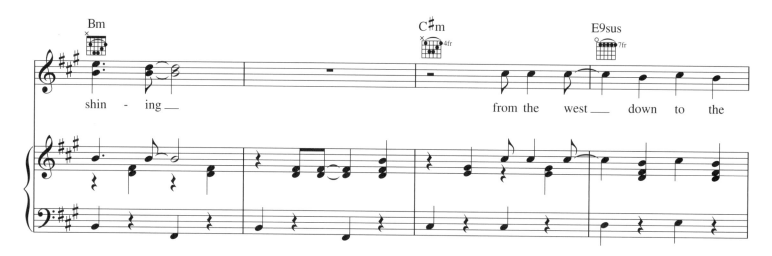

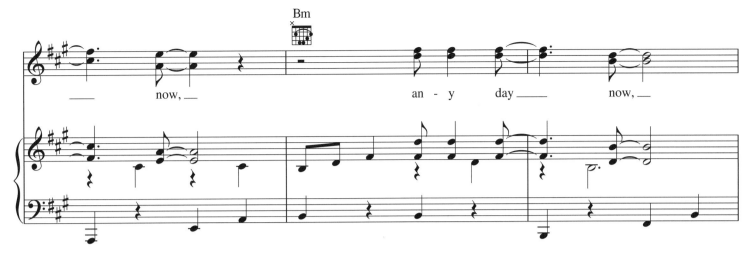

now, _____ an - y day _____ now, ____

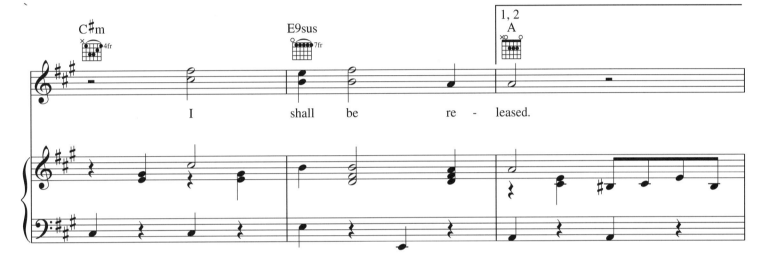

I shall be re - leased.

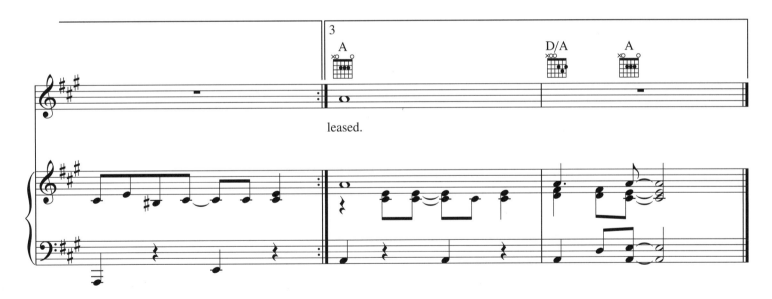

leased.

Additional Lyrics

2. Down here next to me in this lonely crowd
Is a man who swears he's not to blame.
All day long I hear him cry so loud,
Calling out that he's been framed.
Chorus

3. They say ev'rything can be replaced,
Yet ev'ry distance is not near.
So I remember ev'ry face
Of ev'ry man who put me here.
Chorus

I HAD A DREAM

Words and Music by
JOHN SEBASTIAN

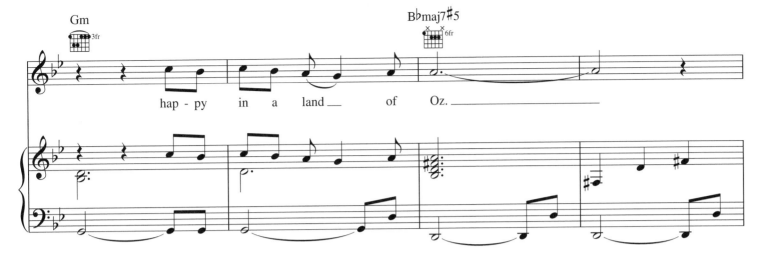

hap - py in a land __ of Oz. _____

Why _____ did ev - 'ry - bod - y laugh __ when I

told them my dream. I _____ guess they

all were __ so far _____ from that kind of scene, _____

feel - in' mean. _____

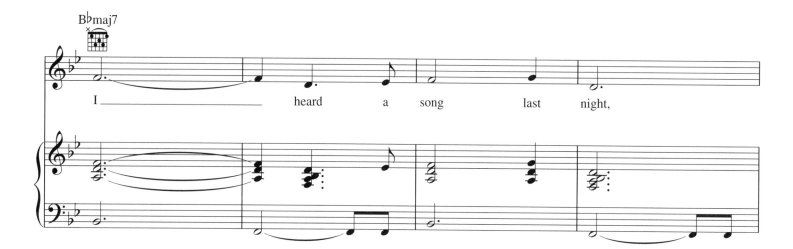

I _____ heard a song last night,

what a love - ly song it was. _____

I thought I'd hum it all night. Un - for -

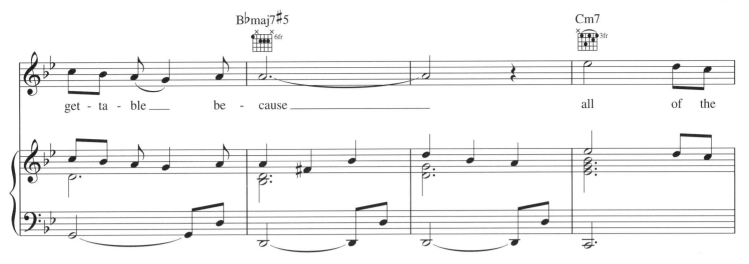

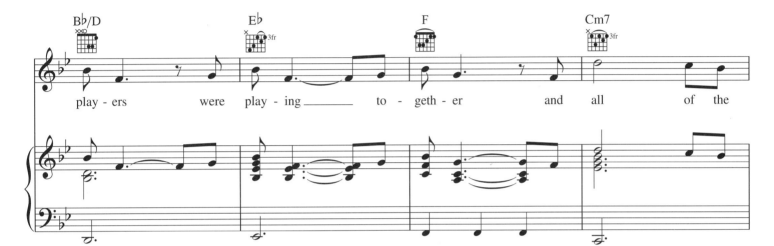

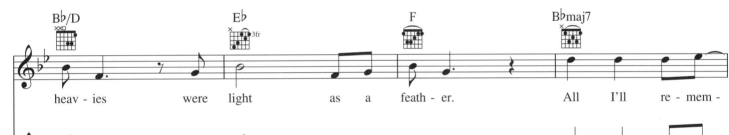

72

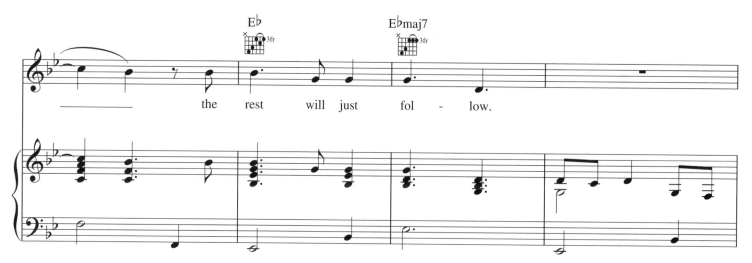

hap - py in a land ___ of Oz. _____

Optional Ending

Repeat and Fade

I'M FREE

Words and Music by
PETE TOWNSHEND

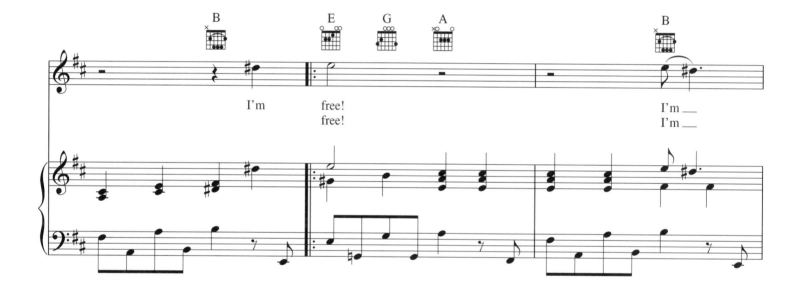

I'm   free!
          free!

I'm ___
I'm ___

free! ___
free! ___

And   free - dom
And I'm wait - ing ___ for

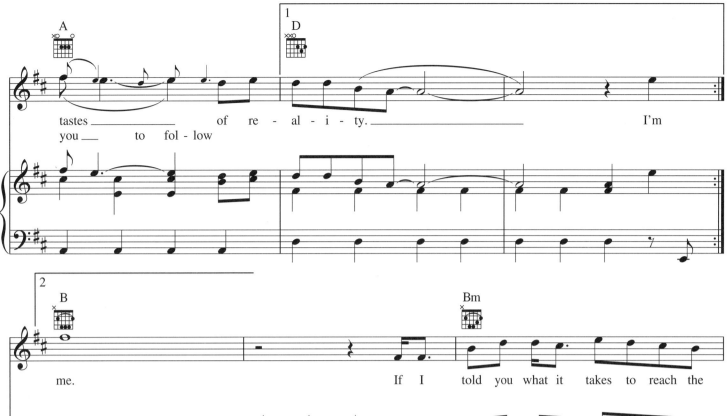

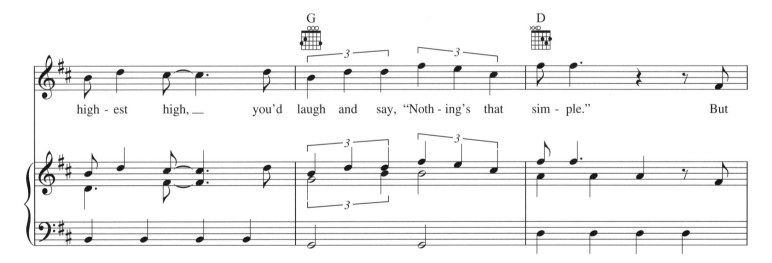

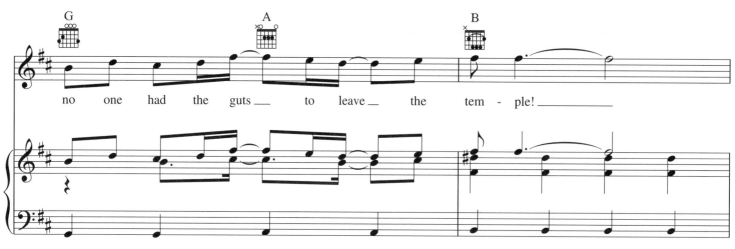

no one had the guts ___ to leave ___ the tem - ple! ___

I'm free! I'm ___

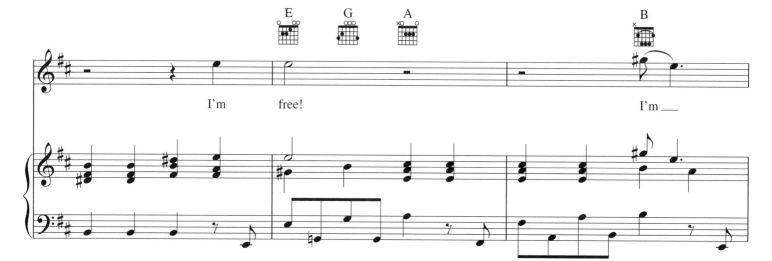

free! ___ And free - dom

tastes ___ of re - al - i - ty. ___ I'm

free!   I'm _____ free! _

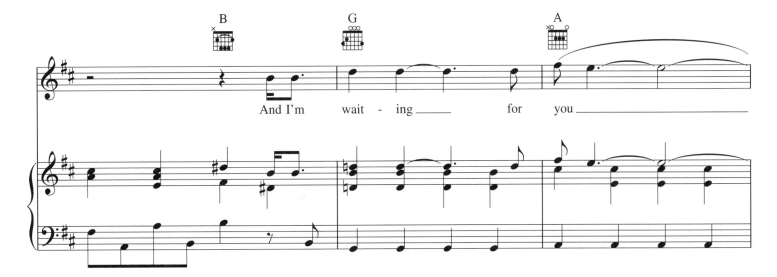

And I'm wait - ing _____ for you _____

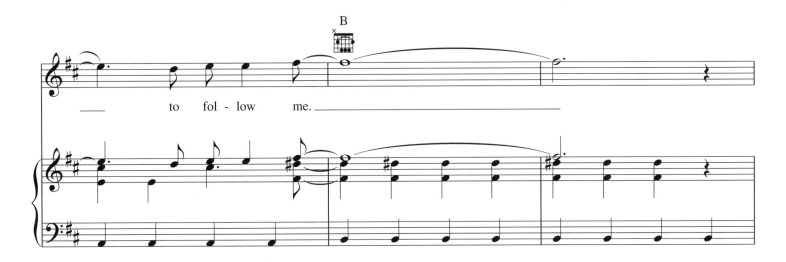

_____ to fol - low me. _____

IF I WERE A CARPENTER

Words and Music by
TIM HARDIN

If I ___ were a car-pen-ter, ___
If I ___ worked my hands in wood, __

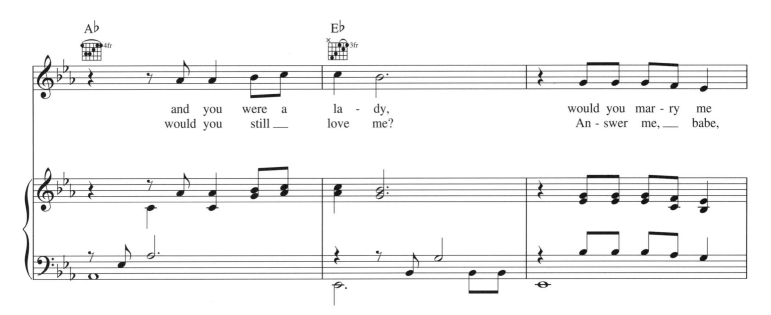

and you were a la- dy,   would you mar-ry me
would you still ___ love me?   An-swer me, ___ babe,

JOE HILL

Words and Music by EARL ROBINSON
and ALFRED HAYES

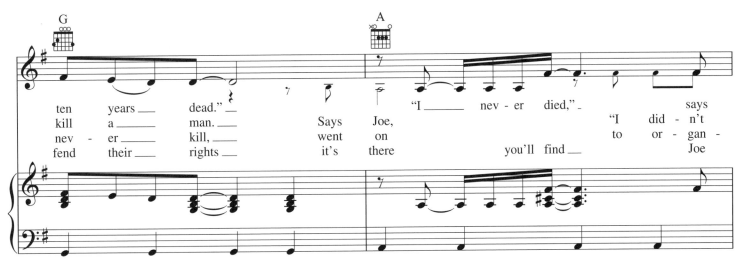

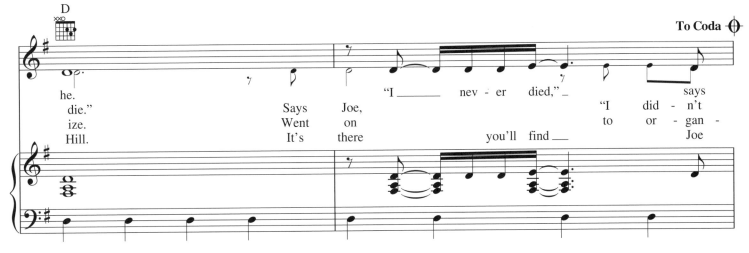

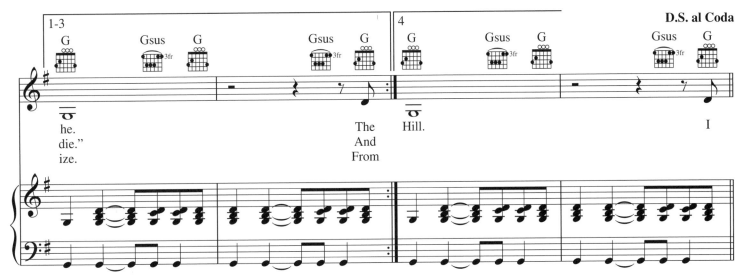

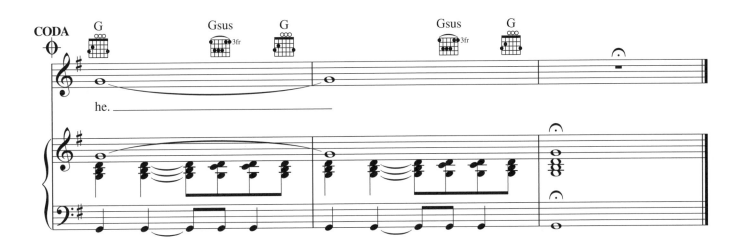

KOZMIC BLUES

Words and Music by JANIS JOPLIN
and GABRIEL MEKLER

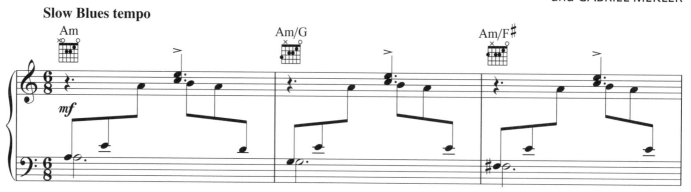

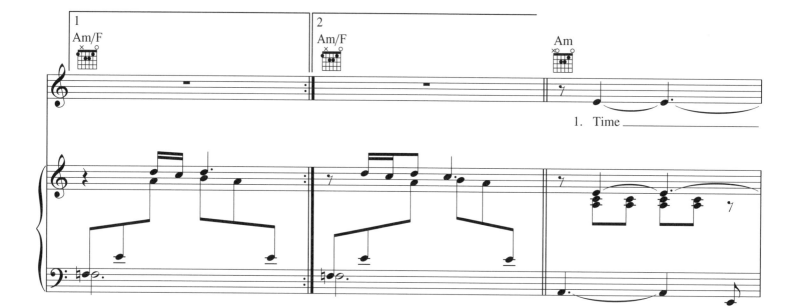

1. Time

keeps mov - in' on,

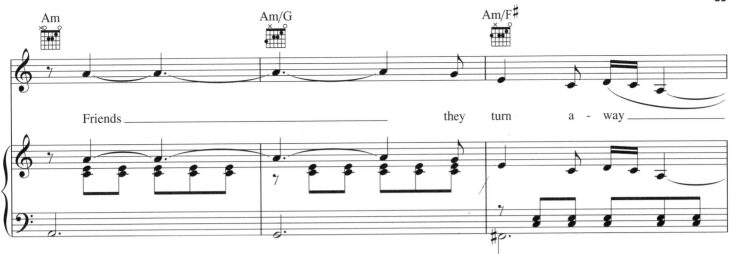

Friends _____ they turn a - way _____

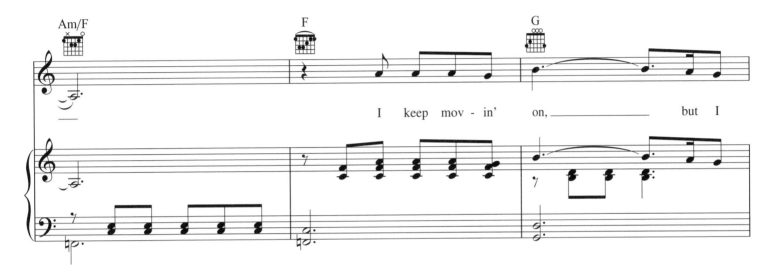

I keep mov - in' on, _____ but I

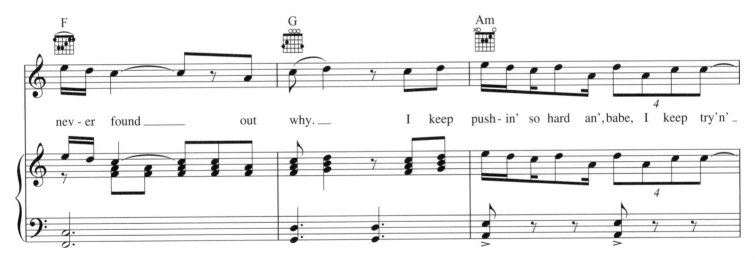

nev - er found _____ out why. ___ I keep push - in' so hard an', babe, I keep try'n' _

___ to make it right to an - oth - er _____ lone - ly day. _____ Well. __

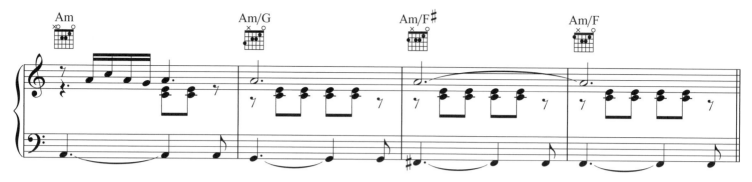

2. Dawn _____ has come at last, _____
3. (See additional lyrics)

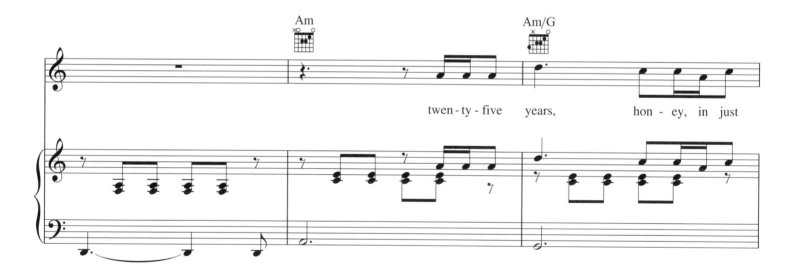

twen - ty - five years, hon - ey, in just

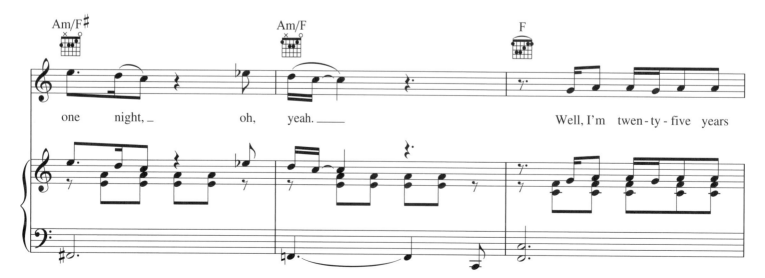

one night, __ oh, yeah. _____ Well, I'm twen-ty-five years

dif- f'rence, babe, ___   I bet-ter hold it now, _   I'm gon-na need it, yeah. _

I bet-ter use it 'til the   day I   die. _____

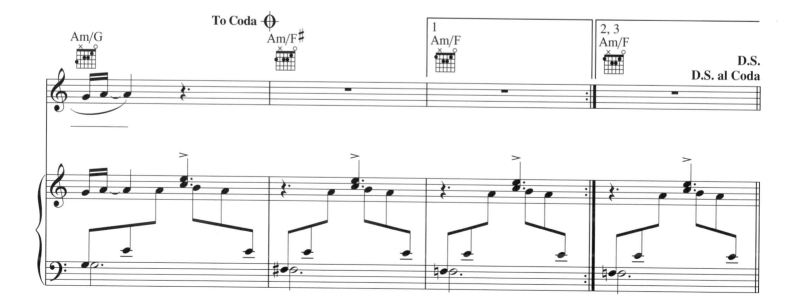

Additional Lyrics

3. Don't expect any answers, dear,
   For, I know that they don't come with age, no, no
   They ain't never gonna love you any better, babe,
   And they're never gonna love you right
   So you better dig it right now, right now, oh.

Chorus 2
Well, it don't make no diff'rence, babe,
And I know, that I can always try
Well, there's a fire inside ev'ry one of us
You're gonna need it now,
I get to hold it, yeah
I'm gonna use it, 'till the day I die.

Chorus 3
Don't make no diff'rence, babe, no, no, no
And it never, ever will
I wanna talk about livin', and lovin', yeah
I get to hold it, babe,
I'm gonna need it now,
I'm gonna use it..

Chorus 4
Don't make no diff'rence, babe,
Oh, honey, I hate to be the one
I said, you better live your life
And, you better love your life
Oh babe, some day you're gonna have to cry
Yes, indeed, yes, indeed.

LET'S GO GET STONED

Words and Music by JOSEPHINE ARMSTEAD,
NICKOLAS ASHFORD and VALERIE SIMPSON

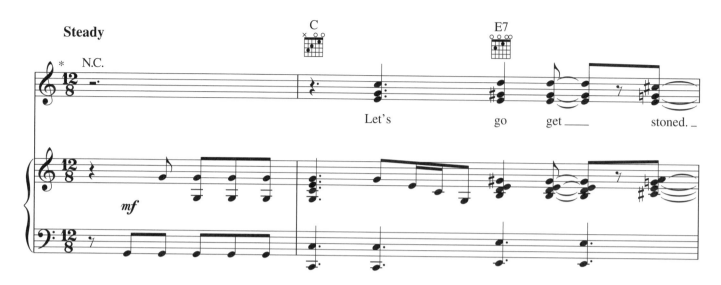

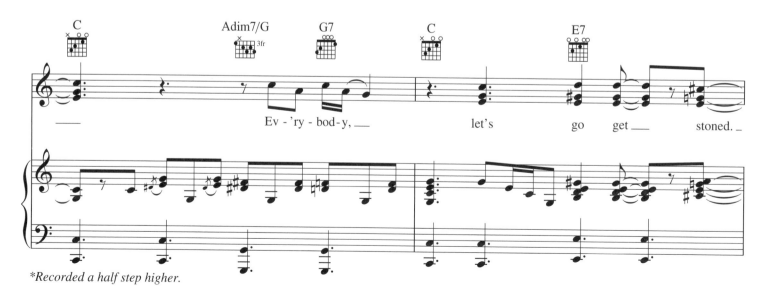

*Recorded a half step higher.

LET'S WORK TOGETHER

Words and Music by
WILBERT HARRISON

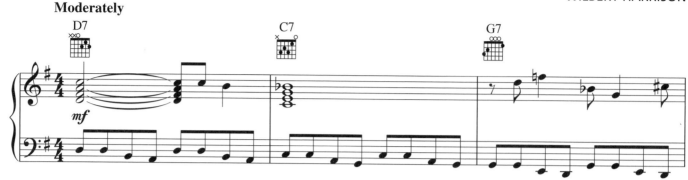

Moderately

To - geth - er we'll stand, ___ di -
things ___ go wrong, ___ as they
two or three min - utes,
make some - one hap - py,

vid - ed we'll fall. ___ Come on now, peo - ple, let's
some - times ___ will and the road you ___ trav - el it stays
two or three hours, ___ what does it mat - ter now in
make some - one smile. ___ Let's all work to - geth - er and make

get on the ball and work to - geth - er.
all up ___ hill, let's work to - geth - er.
this life of ours? Let's work to - geth - er.
life worth - while. Let's work to - geth - er.

Come

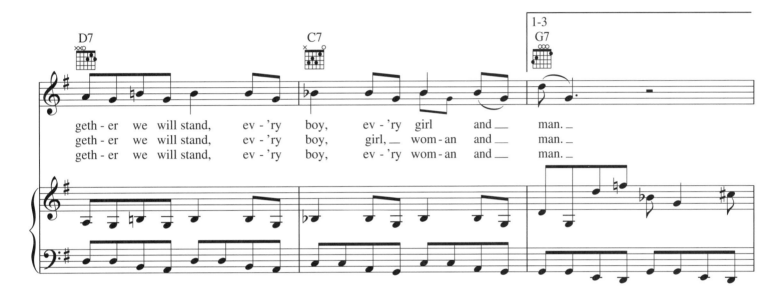

MORE AND MORE

By VEE PEE
and DON JUAN

Moderately fast

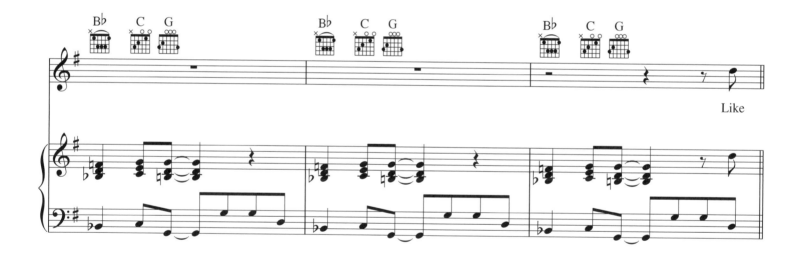

Like

med-i-cine,_ ba - by, you're good for me._ Like hon-ey, dar - lin', yeah,_____ I

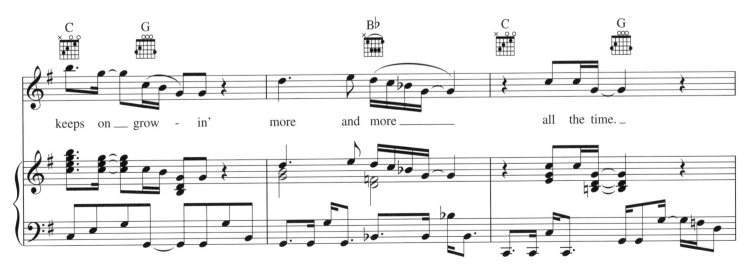

More and more _____ all the time. _

Like a

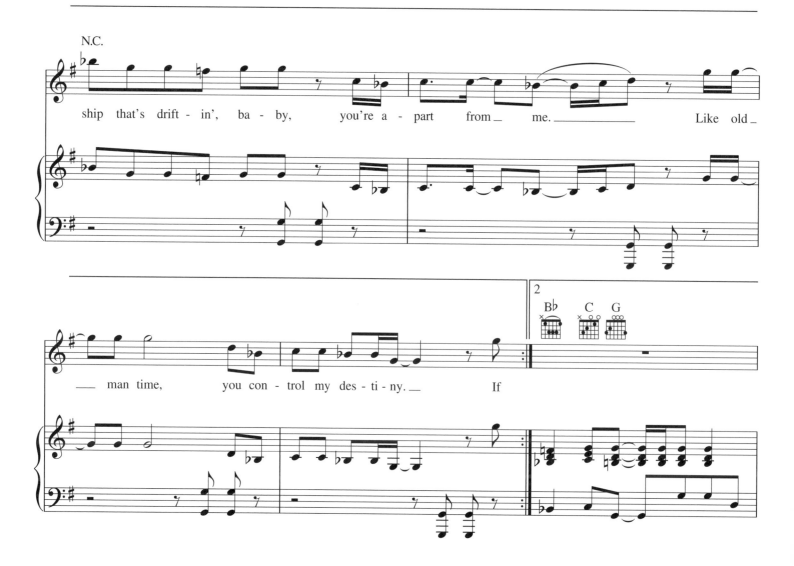

ship that's drift - in', ba - by, you're a - part from _ me. _____ Like old _

_____ man time, you con - trol my des - ti - ny. _ If

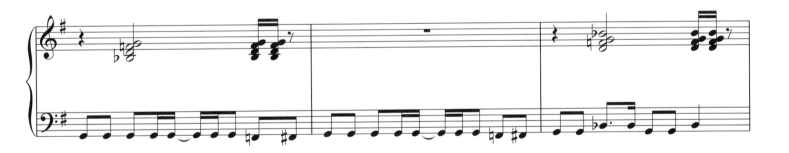

N.C.

Sure as the

sun - rise, _____ I'll stand by your side. _____

Sure as the day - break, _ I'll love you for heav-en's sake. _____

I'm read - y to pay, _ yeah, my dues for lov - in' you. _

For lov-in' you too much, wom-an, you know I stand_ ac-cused._____

More, more, all the time._ More and more._

MY GENERATION

Words and Music by
PETER TOWNSHEND

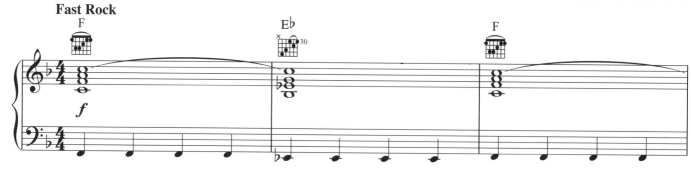

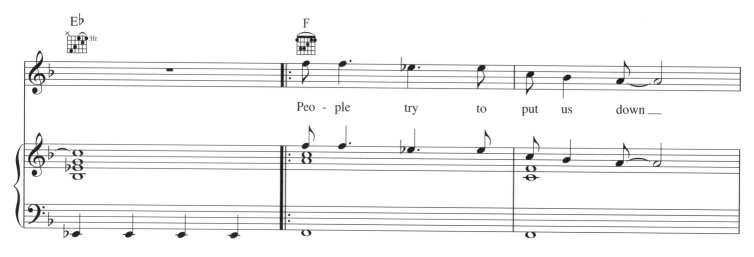

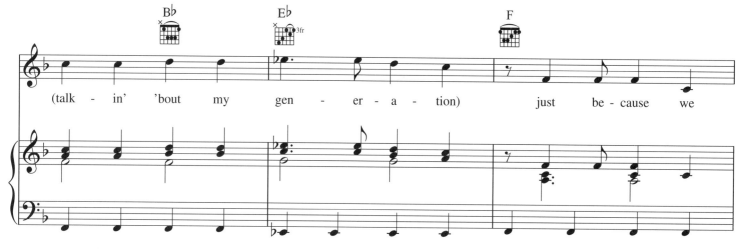

105

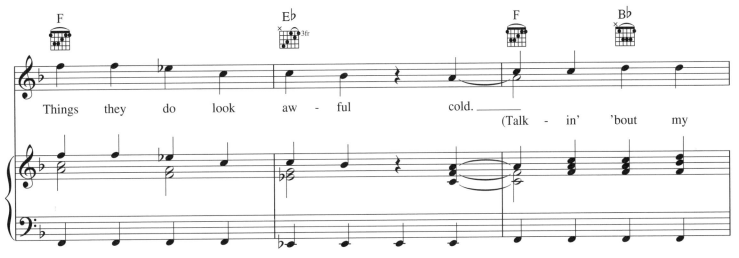

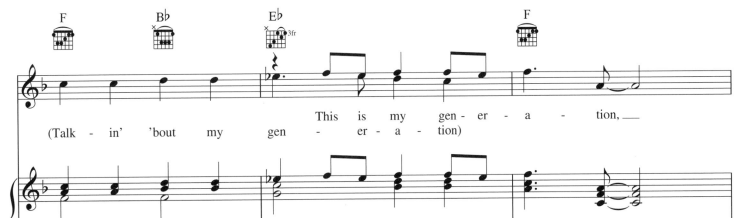

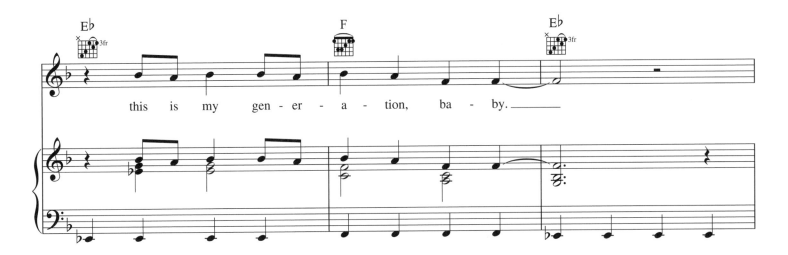

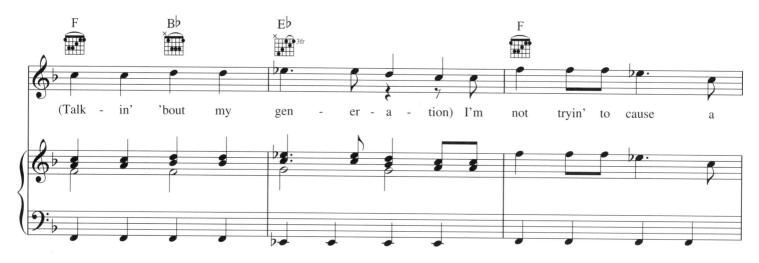

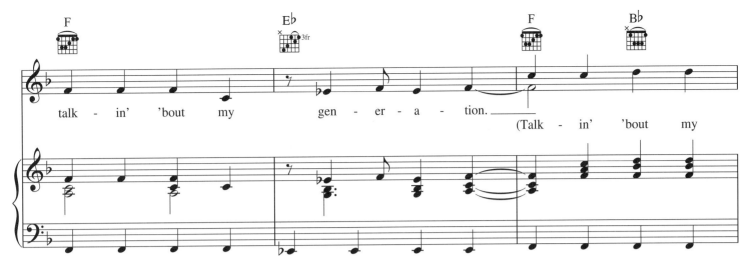

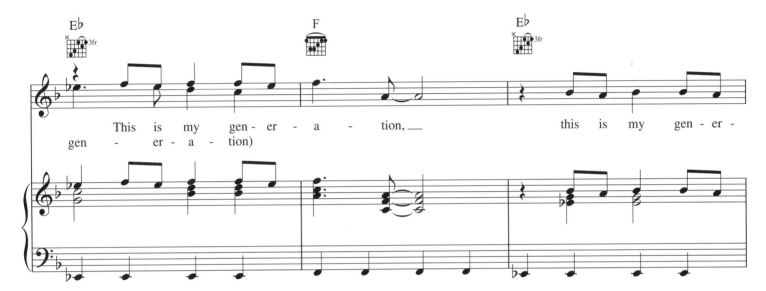

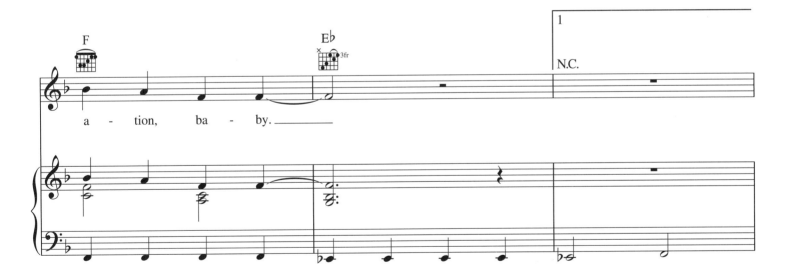

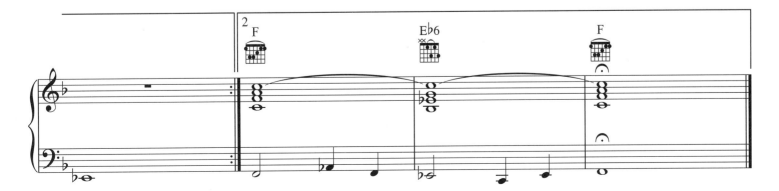

NIGHT TIME IS THE RIGHT TIME

Words and Music by ROOSEVELT SYKES
and JAMES ODEN

night and day, night and day, night and day,

A♭7

E♭7

night and day, night and day, night and day,

B♭7

A♭7

night and day, night and day, night and day,

E♭7

night and day,

1
night and day.

2
night and day. __

PERSUASION

Words and Music by
GREGG ROLIE

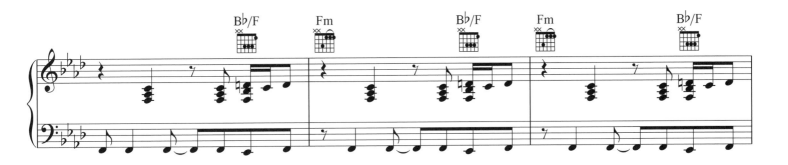

You _____ got per-sua-sion.

I _____ can't help my-self. _____ You _____ got per-

suā - sion.   I _____   can't help my -

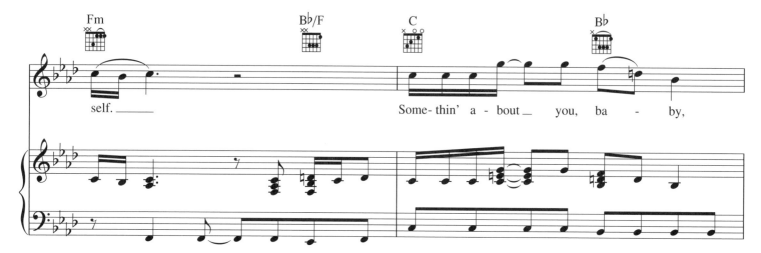

self. _____   Some-thin' a - bout __ you, ba - by,

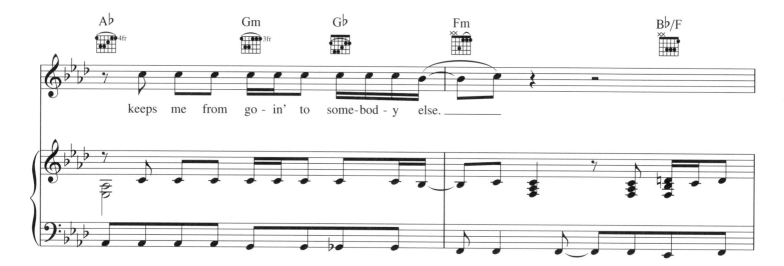

keeps me from go - in' to some-bod - y else. _____

Now the   way _____ you walk __ now,   now, now
spell you've put on me ___ has   just out -

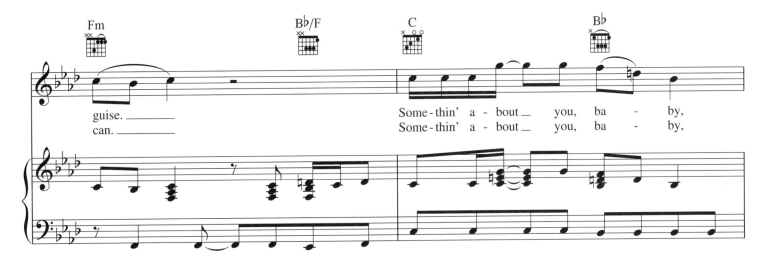

you're one, ___ you're one of a kind. ___
make me feel, make me feel like a man. ___

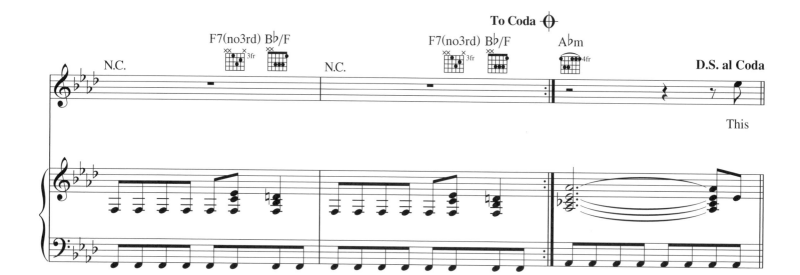

This

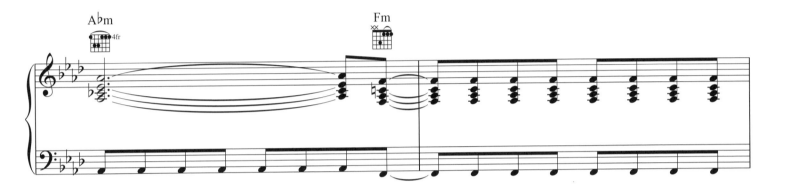

PIECE OF MY HEART

Words and Music by BERT BERNS
and JERRY RAGOVOY

Slowly, with a beat

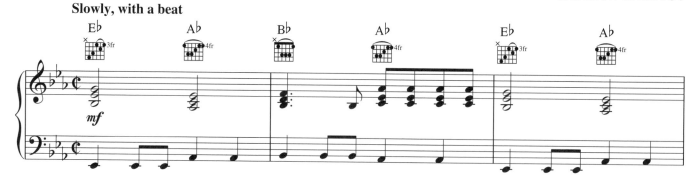

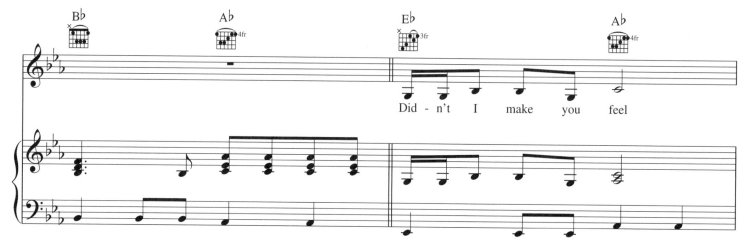

Did-n't I make you feel

like you were the on - ly man, ___

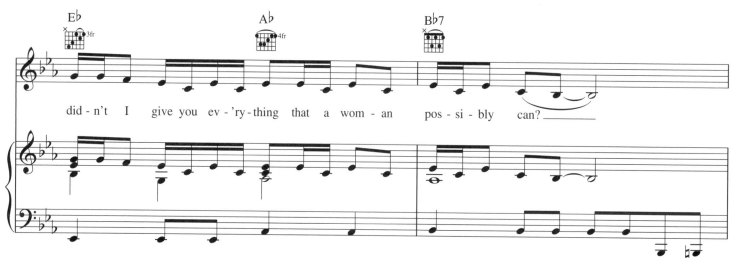

did-n't I give you ev-'ry-thing that a wom-an pos-si-bly can? ___

But with all the love I give you, it's nev-er e-nough, __ but

I'm gon-na show you, ba-by, that a wom-an can be tough. __ So

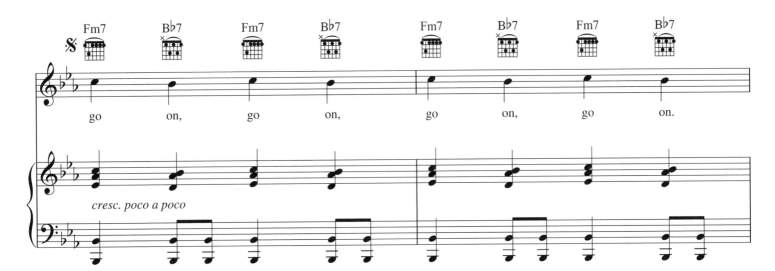

go on, go on, go on, go on.

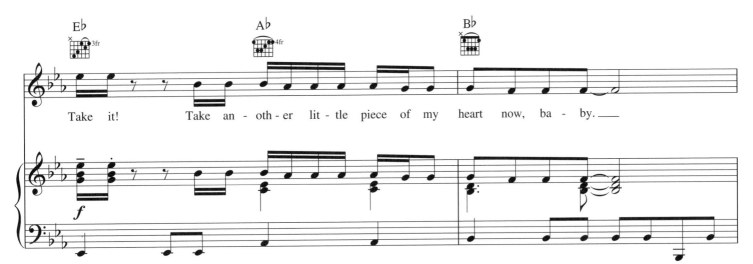

Take it! Take an-oth-er lit-tle piece of my heart now, ba-by. __

And, oh _____ you nev-er, nev-er hear me when I cry at night. __

Whoa-oh - oh, ____ I tell my-self that I can't stand the pain, but when you

hold me in your arms I say it a-gain. __ So

D.S. al Coda

CODA

You know you got it if it makes you feel good. __

PROUD MARY

Words and Music by
JOHN FOGERTY

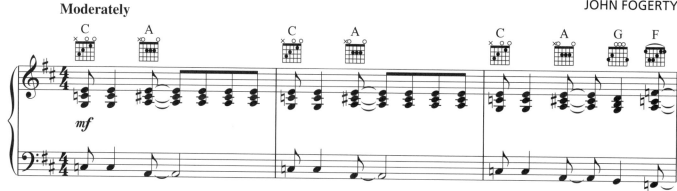

Left a good job __ in the cit - y,   work-in' for the man __ ev - 'ry
Cleaned a lot of plates __ in Mem - phis,   pumped a lot of 'tane __ down in
If you come down __ to the riv - er,   bet you gon - na find __ some __

night and   day. __   And I nev - er lost __ one min - ute of sleep - in',
New Or - leans. __   But I nev - er saw __ the good __ side of the cit - y
peo - ple who live.   You don't have to wor - ry __ 'cause __ you have no mon - ey.

wor - ry'n''bout the way ___ things ___ might have ___ been. ___
till I hitched a ride ___ on a ___ riv - er - boat ___ queen.
Peo - ple on the riv - er are ___ hap - py to ___ give.

Big wheel, ___ keep on turn -

- in', ___ proud ___ Mar - y keep on burn - in'. Roll - in', ___ roll -

1
To Coda ⊕

- in', ___ roll - in' on the riv - er. ___

2

- in' on the riv - er. ___

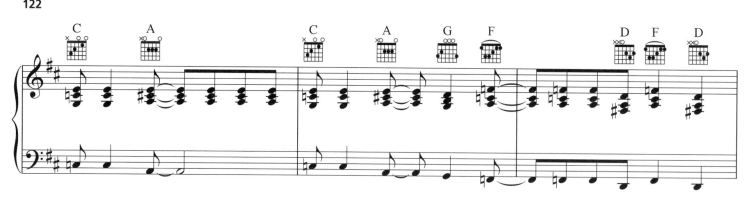

Roll - in', roll -

- in', roll - in' on the riv - er. _____

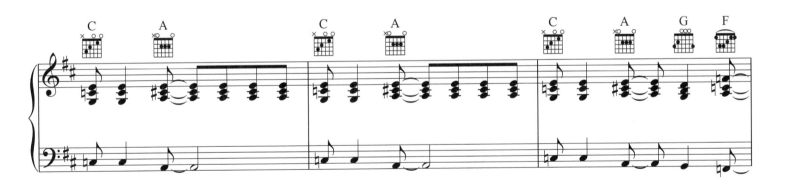

D.S. al Coda

CODA

in' on the riv - er._____ Roll - in', roll -

Repeat and Fade

- in', roll - in' on the riv - er._____ Roll -

Optional Ending

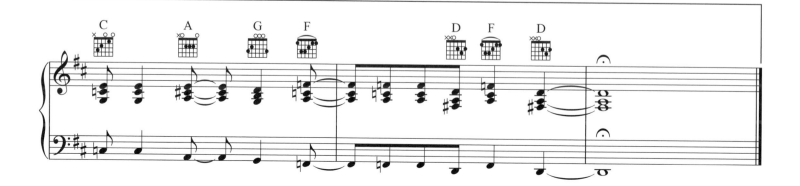

SOMEBODY TO LOVE

Words and Music by
DARBY SLICK

With a steady beat

When the truth is found _ to be _

_ lies, and all _ the joy _

with - in you _ dies, don't you _

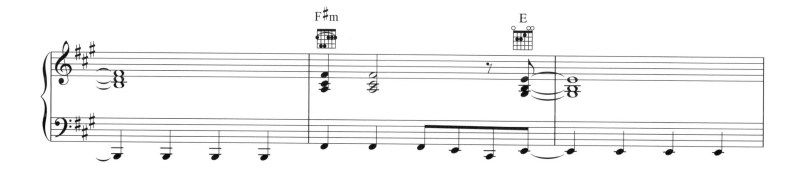

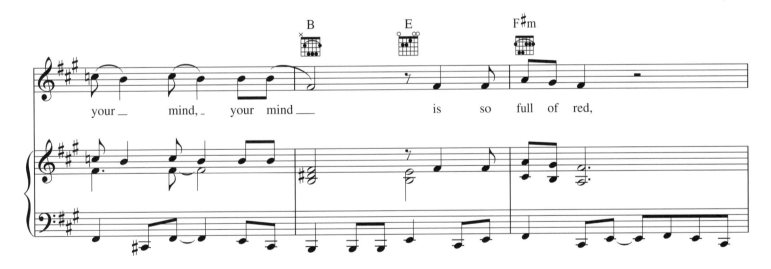

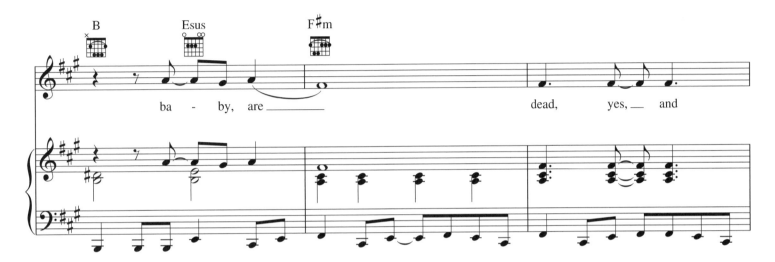

Tears _ are run - ning, _____ they're _ all run -

- ning down your breast, and your friends, ba - by,

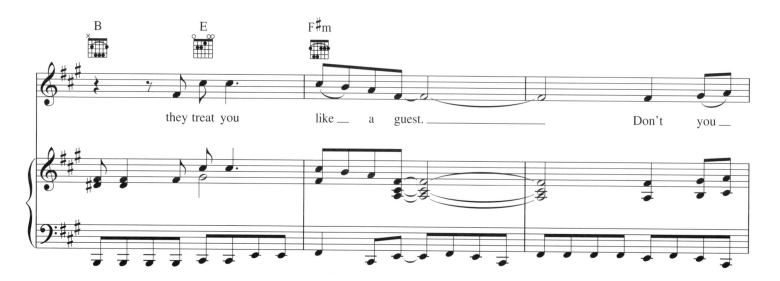

they treat you like _ a guest. _____ Don't you _

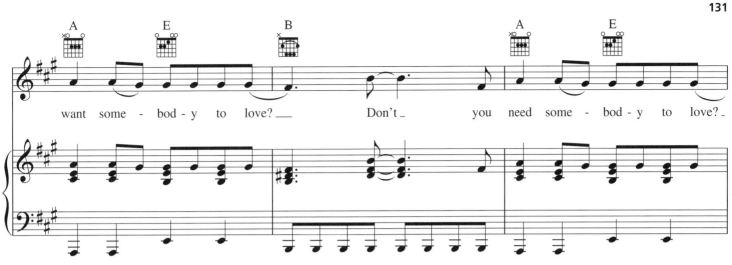

want some-bod-y to love? ___ Don't ___ you need some-bod-y to love? ___

___ Would-n't you ___ love some-bod-y to love? ___ You bet-ter find ___

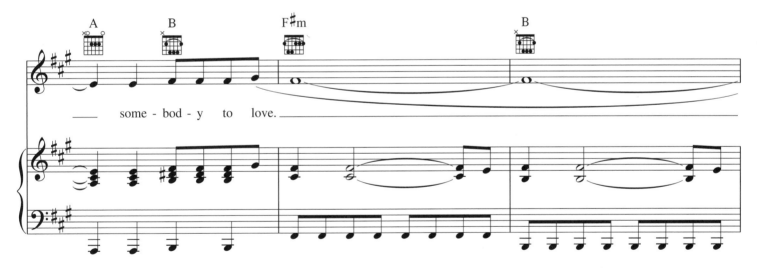

___ some-bod-y to love. ___

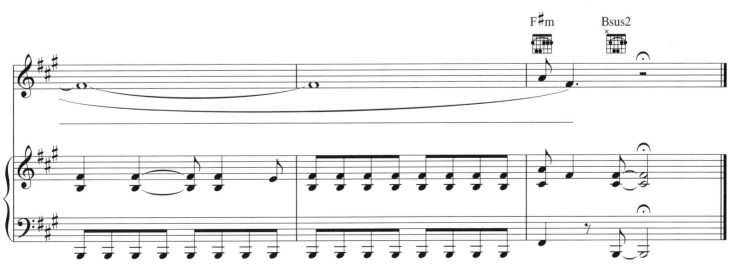

SOUL SACRIFICE

By CARLOS SANTANA

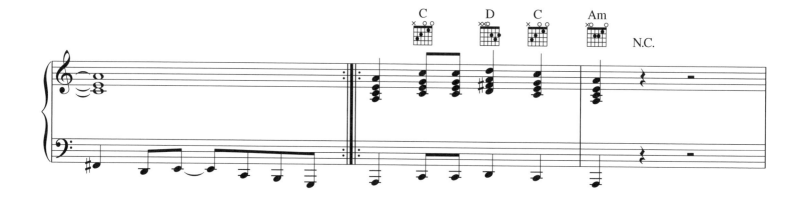

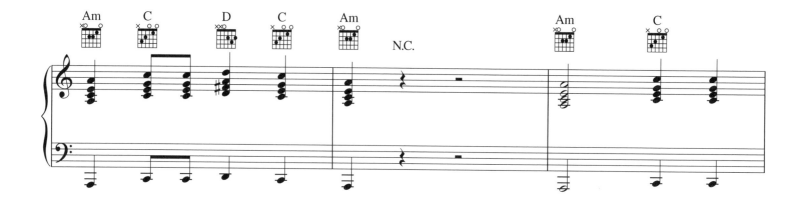

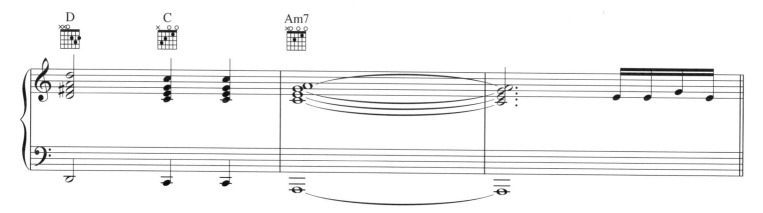

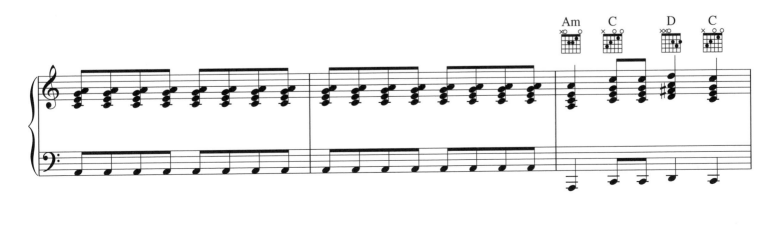

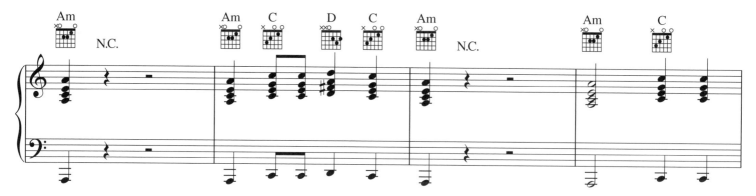

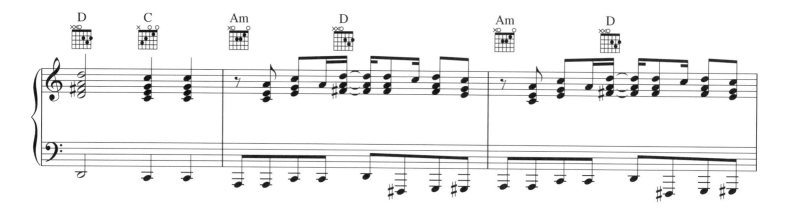

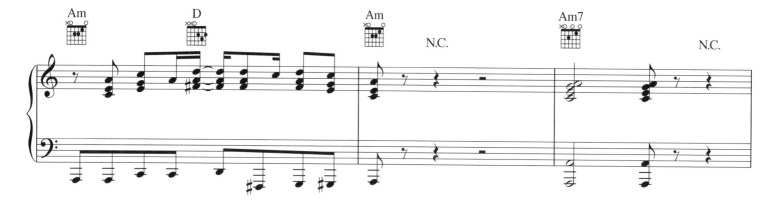

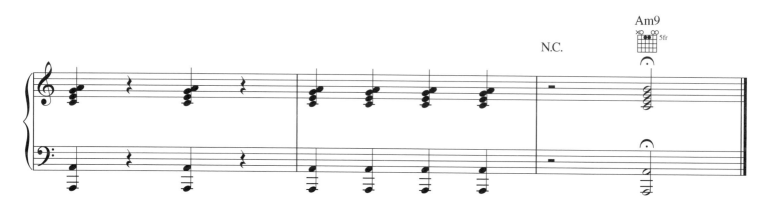

SUITE: JUDY BLUE EYES

Words and Music by
STEPHEN STILLS

It's get-ting to __ the point __ where I'm no
mem-ber what __ we've said __ and done and

fun an-y-more. __ I am sor-ry.
felt a-bout each oth — er. Oh, babe, have mer — cy.

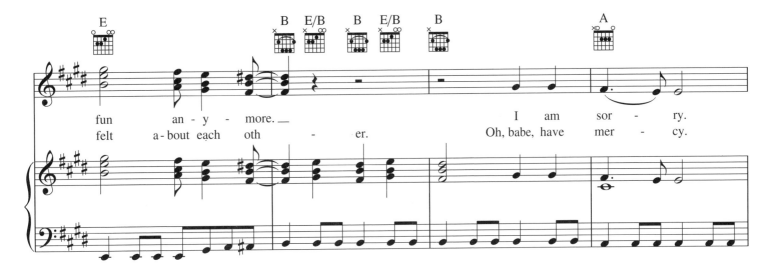

Some - times it hurts ___ so bad - ly I
Don't let the past ___ re - mind us of

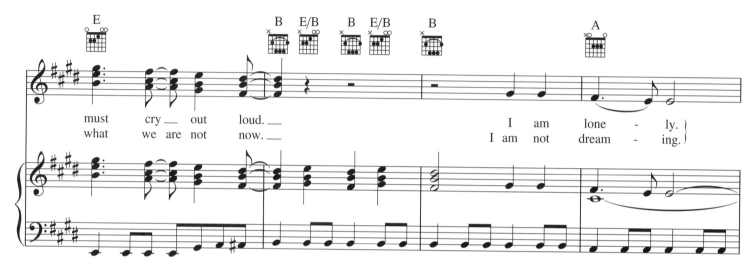

must cry ___ out loud. ___ I am lone - ly.
what we are not now. ___ I am not dream - ing.

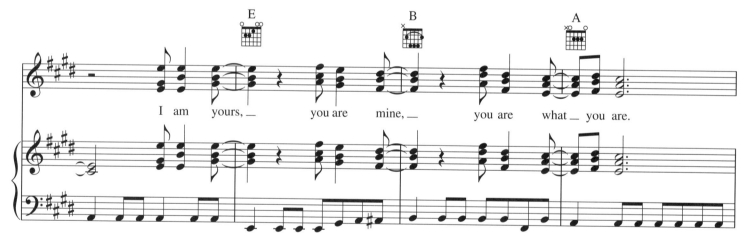

I am yours, ___ you are mine, ___ you are what ___ you are.

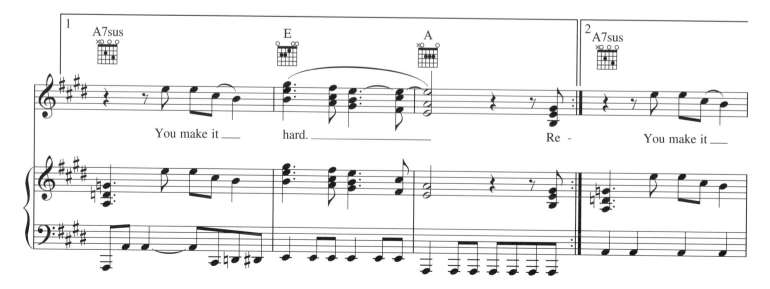

You make it ___ hard. _____ Re - You make it ___

hard.

Tear - ing your - self

a - way ___ from ___ me now, _____ you are free _____

and I ___ am cry - ing. ___ This does ___ not

mean _ I don't love you, _ I do, ___ that's for - ev - er, _

yes, and _ for al - ways. ____ I am yours, _

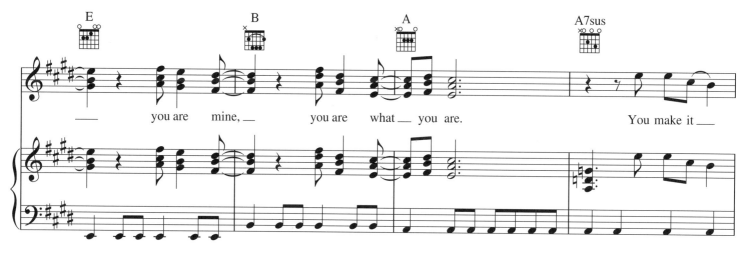

_ you are mine, _ you are what _ you are. You make it _

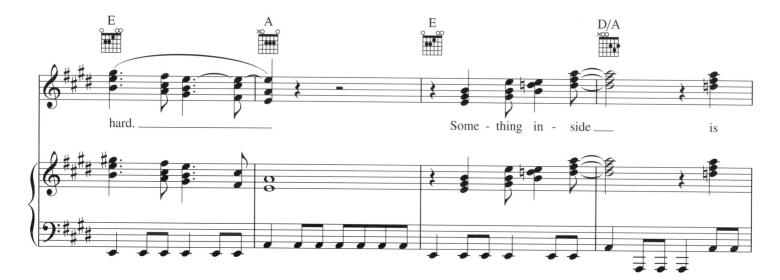

hard. _____ Some - thing in - side _ is

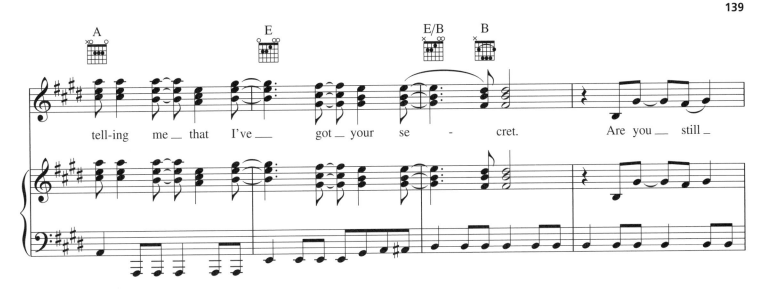

tell-ing me ___ that I've ___ got ___ your se - cret. Are you ___ still ___

lis - t'ning? Fear is ___ the lock ___ and

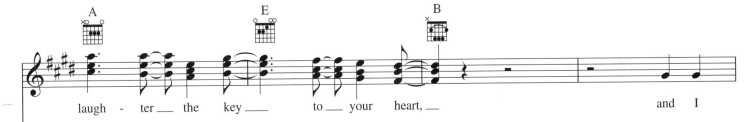

laugh - ter ___ the key ___ to ___ your heart, ___ and I

love ___ you. I am yours, ___ you are mine, ___ you are what ___

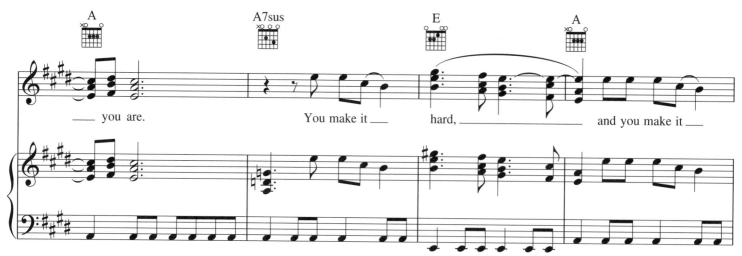

you are. You make it ___ hard, _____ and you make it ___

hard, _____ and you make it ___ hard, _____

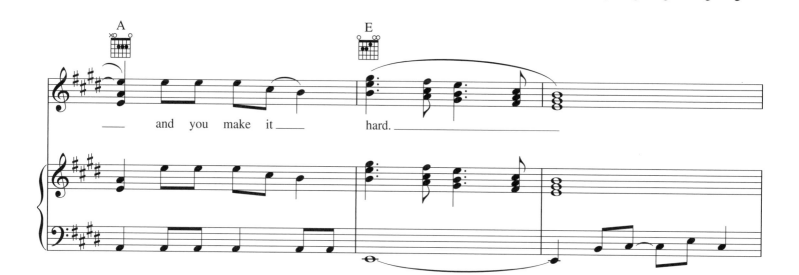

___ and you make it ___ hard. _____

tell it like it is? _____ But lis - ten to me, ba - by. _____

It's my heart ____ that's a - suf - f'rin'. It's a - dy - in'. And that's ____ what I _____ have to

lose.

I've _____ got an an - swer.
Will _____ you come see _____ me _____

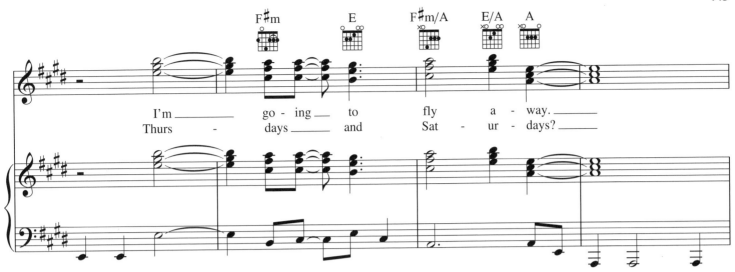

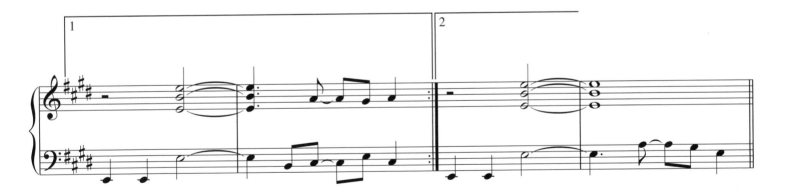

Chest-nut - brown _ ca - nar - - y, _____ ru - by - throat - ed spar -
Voic - es of _____ the an - - gels, _____ ring a - round _ the moon -
Lac - y, lilt - ing lyr - ic, _____ los - ing love, _ la - ment -

row,   sing   a   song,   don't   be   long,
light,   ask - ing me, said   she   so   free,
ing,   change   my   life,   make   it   right,

thrill   me   to   the   mar - row.
"How   can you catch the spar - row?"
be   my   la - dy.

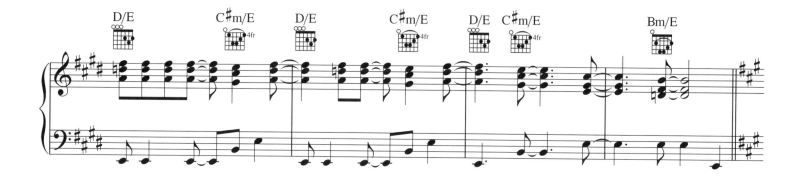

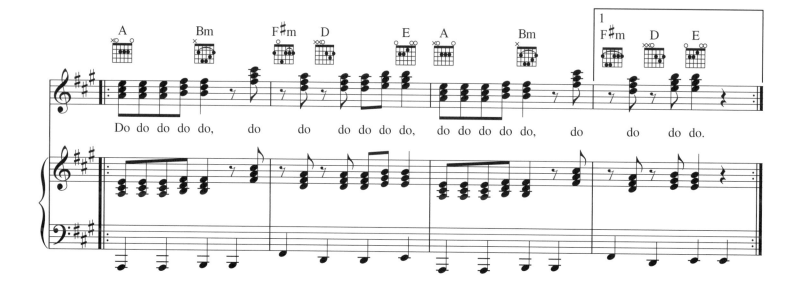

Do do do do do,   do   do   do do do do,   do do do do do,   do   do   do do.

SPINNING WHEEL

Words and Music by
DAVID CLAYTON THOMAS

Moderately slow, with a beat

What goes up must come down, spin-ning wheel got to go 'round. Talk-in' 'bout your trou-bles, it's a

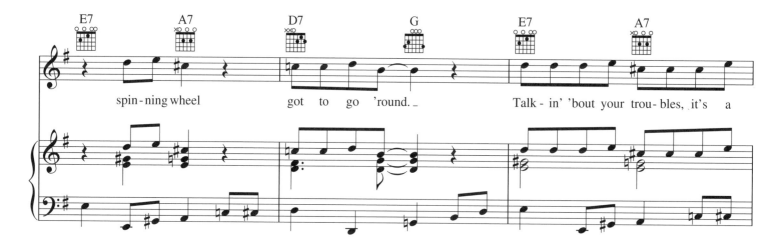

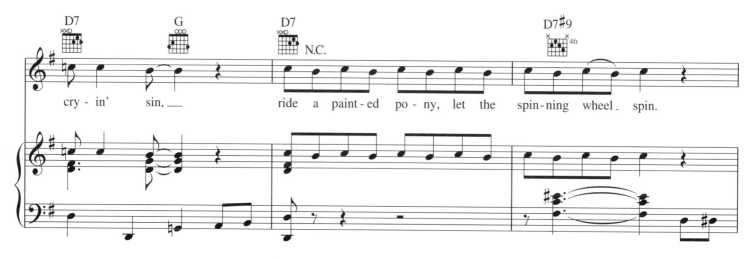

cry-in' sin, ride a paint-ed po-ny, let the spin-ning wheel spin.

straight and nar - row high - way. ___ Would you mind ___ a re -

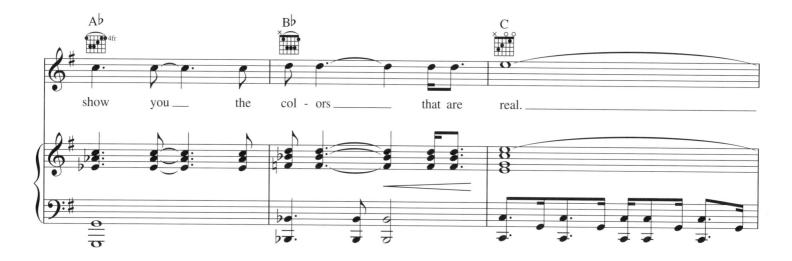

flect - ing sign? ___ Just let it shine ___ with - in your mind, ___ and

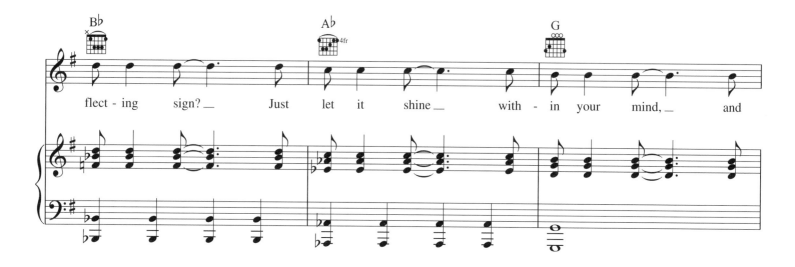

show you ___ the col - ors ___ that are real. ___

Some-one is wait - ing just for you, _____ spin-ning wheel

spin - ning true. _____ Drop all your trou - bles by the riv - er - side, _____

catch a paint - ed po - ny on the spin - ning wheel ___ ride.

Repeat and Fade

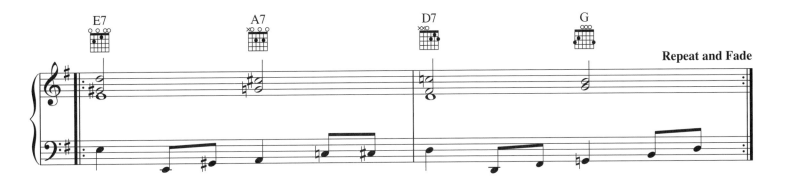

STRAWBERRY FIELDS FOREVER

Words and Music by JOHN LENNON
and PAUL McCARTNEY

Let me take you down, ___ 'cause I'm go-ing to ___

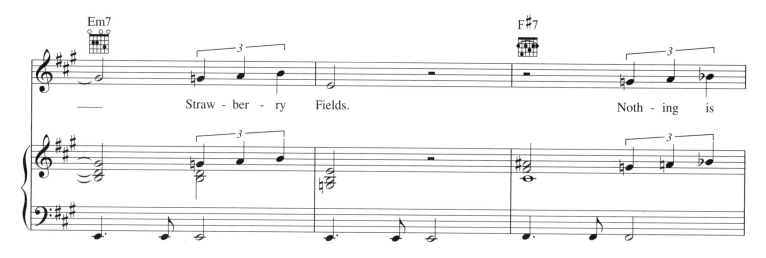

___ Straw-ber-ry Fields.

Noth-ing is

real, and noth-ing to get hung a-bout.

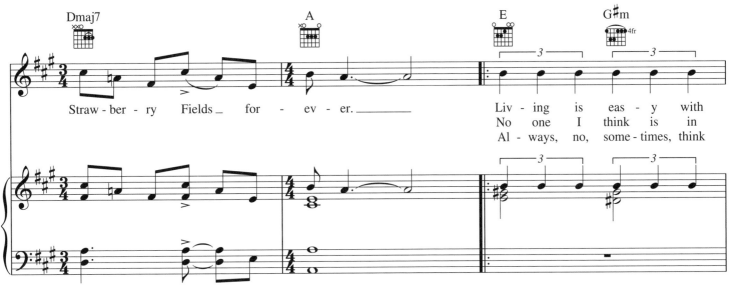

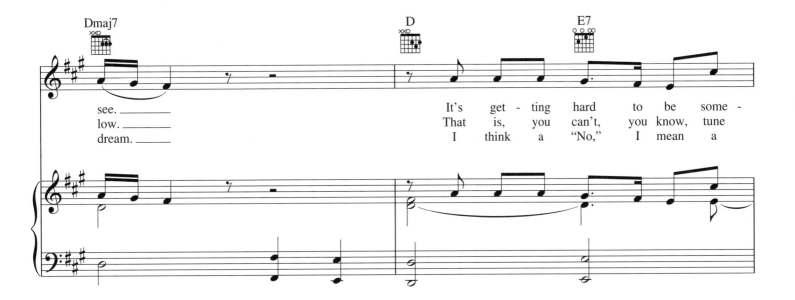

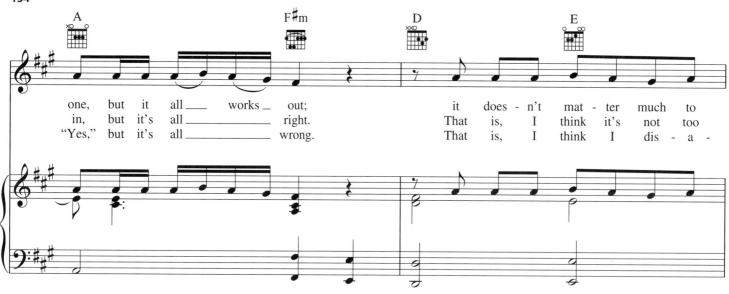

one, but it all ___ works ___ out; it does-n't mat-ter much to
in, but it's all _____ right. That is, I think it's not too
"Yes," but it's all _____ wrong. That is, I think I dis-a-

me.
bad. }
gree.

Let me take you down, ___ 'cause I'm go-ing to ___

___ Straw-ber-ry Fields. Noth-ing is real, and

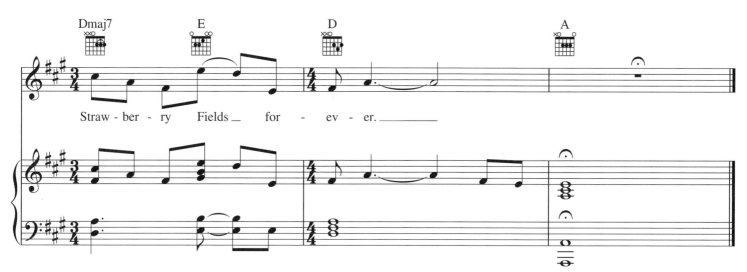

SUSIE-Q

Words and Music by DALE HAWKINS,
STAN LEWIS and ELEANOR BROADWATER

(1.,4.) Oh, _____ Su - sie Q. _____

(2.) *Instrumental solo*

Solo ends (3.) Well, say that you'll be true. _____

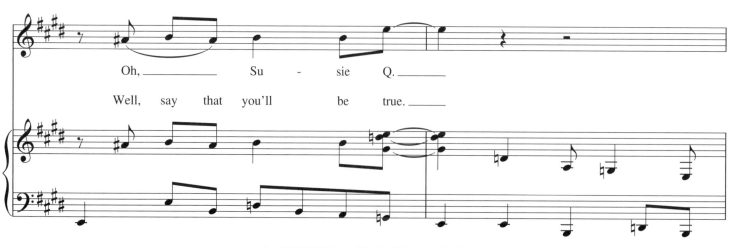

Oh, _____ Su - sie Q. _____

Well, say that you'll be true. _____

Oh, _____ Su - sie Q, _____ ba - by, I love ____ you, _

Solo continues

Well, say that you'll be true _____ and nev - er leave me _____ blue, _

____ Su - sie Q. _____ I like the way you walk. _

____ Su - sie Q. _____ Well, say that you'll be mine. _

____ I like the way you talk. _

____ Well, say that you'll be mine. _

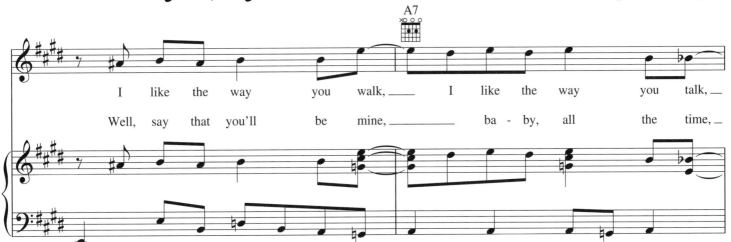

I like the way you walk, ____ I like the way you talk, _

Well, say that you'll be mine, _____ ba - by, all the time, _

158

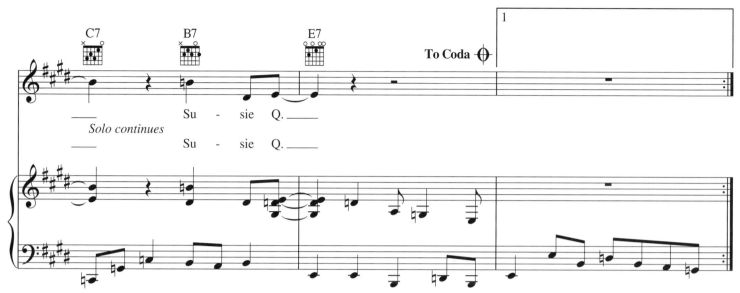

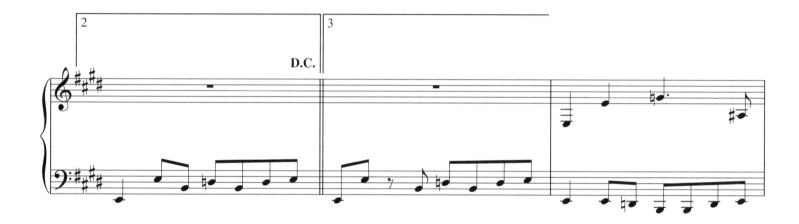

Oh,   Su - sie   Q. _____

Oh, Su - sie Q. _____ Oh, Su - sie Q, _

_____ mm, ba - by, I love you, _____ Su - sie Q. _____

Instrumental solo

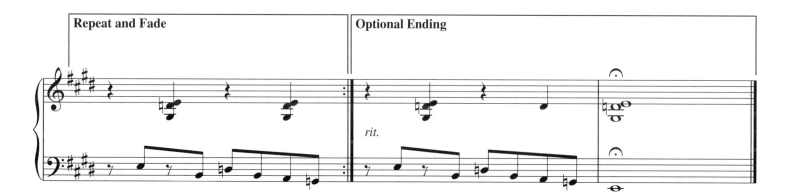

Repeat and Fade

Optional Ending

rit.

THEME FOR AN IMAGINARY WESTERN

Words and Music by JACK BRUCE
and PETE BROWN

Moderately slow

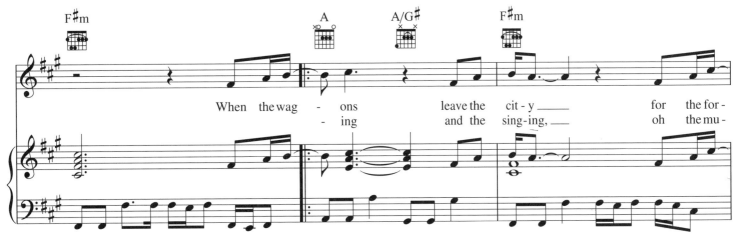

When the wag - ons leave the cit - y _____ for the for-
- ing and the sing-ing, _____ oh the mu -

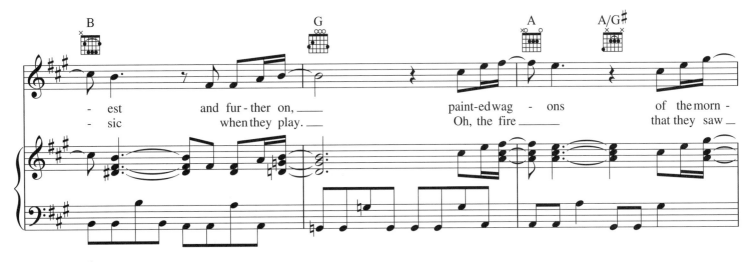

- est and fur-ther on, _____ paint-ed wag - ons of the morn -
- sic when they play. _____ Oh, the fire _____ that they saw _____

- ing, dust - y roads where they have gone. _____ Some - times
_____ there on the trail with no re - gret. _____ Some-times they

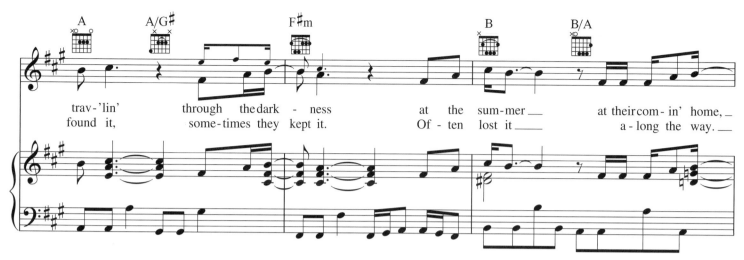

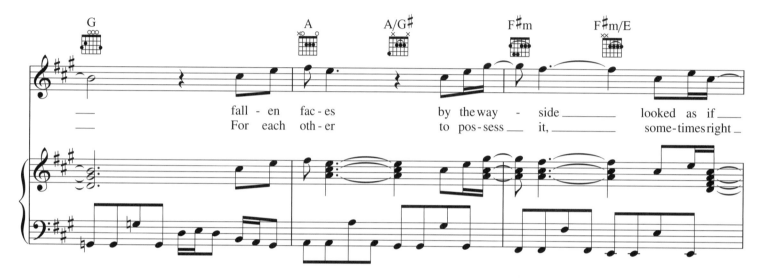

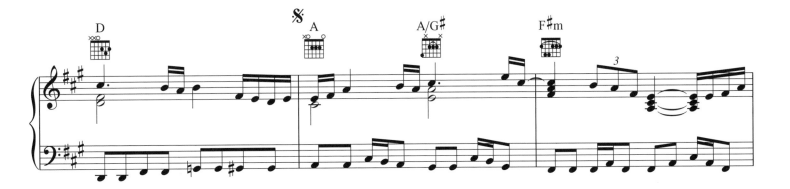

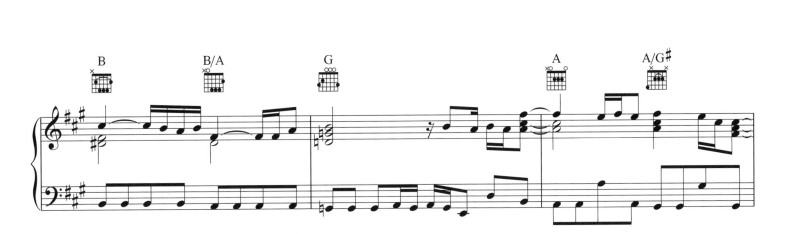

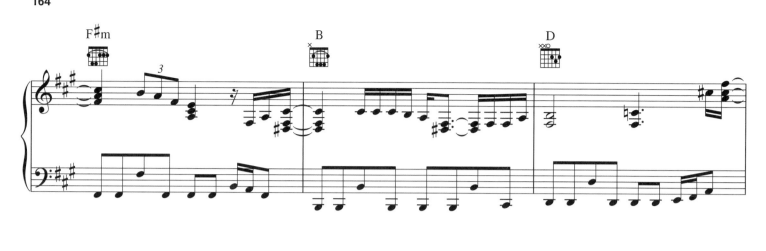

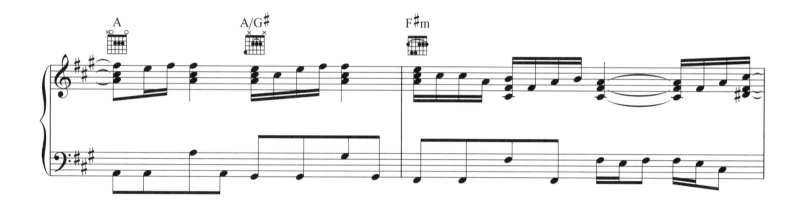

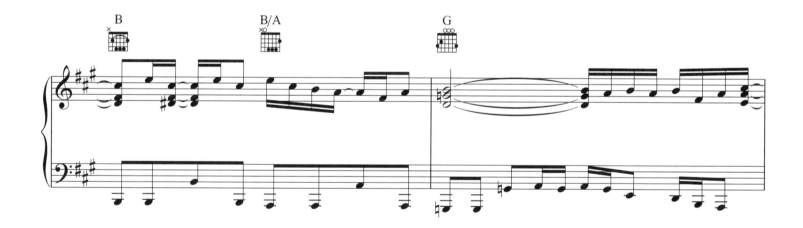

Oh, the sun _____ was in their eyes, __

and the de - sert that's dry _____ in the

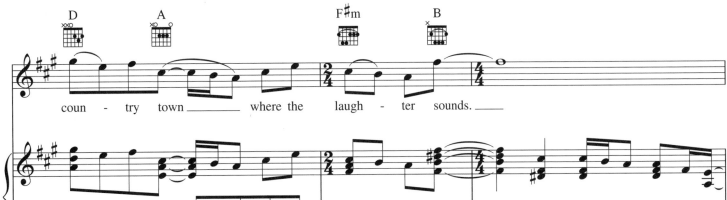

coun - try town _____ where the laugh - ter sounds. ____

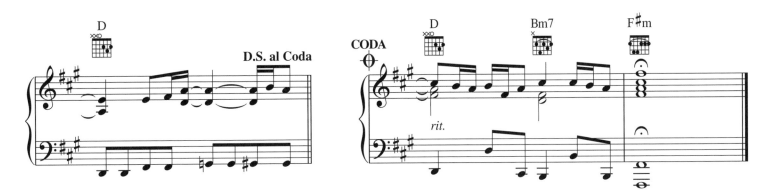

D.S. al Coda

CODA

rit.

TURN ON YOUR LOVE LIGHT

Words and Music by DON ROBEY
and JOE SCOTT

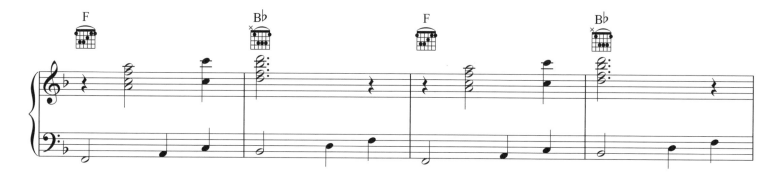

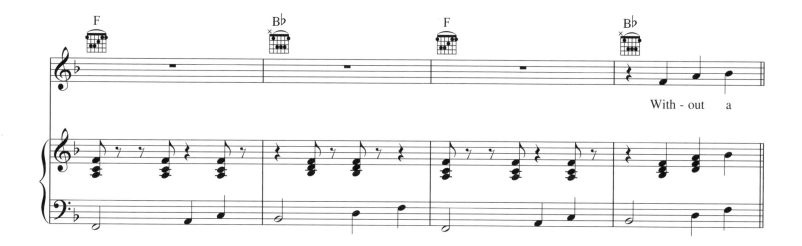

With - out a

warn - in' ____ you broke ____ my heart. ____

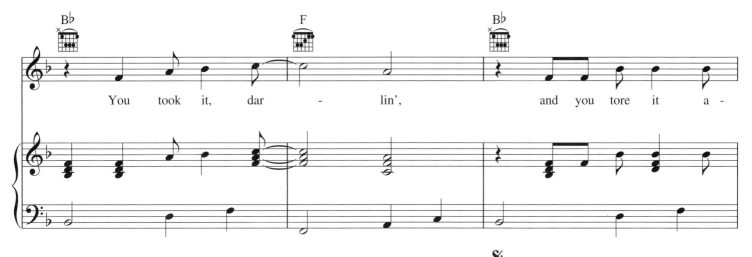

You took it, dar - lin', and you tore it a -

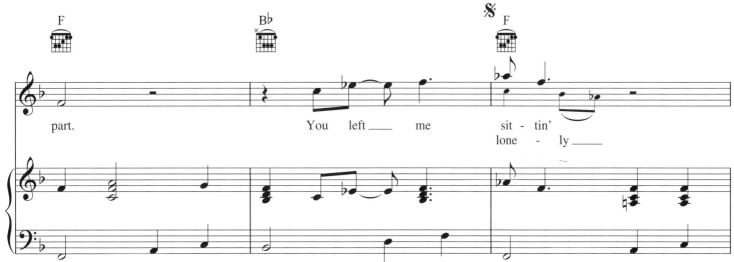

part. You left ____ me sit - tin'
lone - ly ____

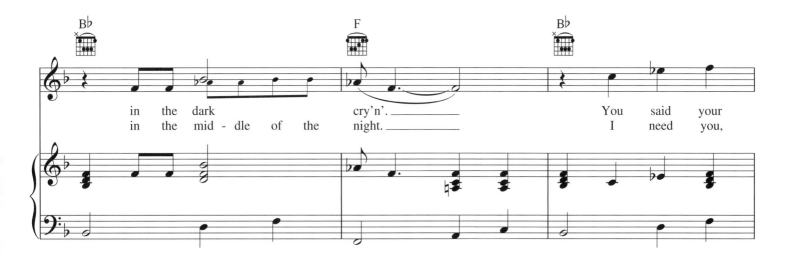

in the dark cry'n'. ____
in the mid - dle of the night. ____

You said your
I said need you,

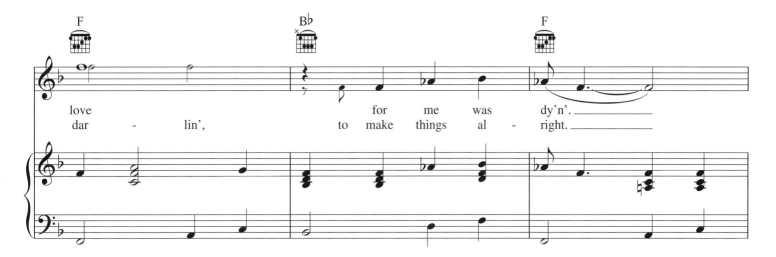

love
dar - lin',

for me was dy'n'. ____
to make things al - right. ____

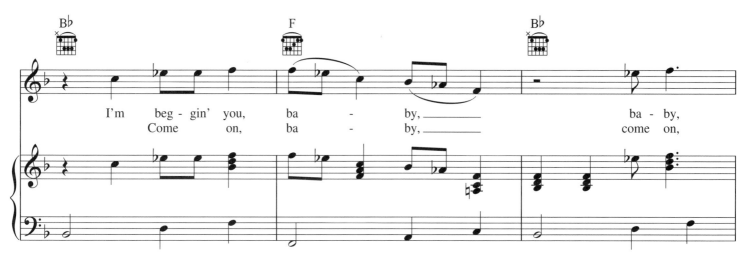

I'm beg - gin' you, ba - by, _____ ba - by,
Come on, ba - by, _____ come on,

please. _____ I'm beg - gin' you, ba - by,
please. _____ Come on, ba - by,

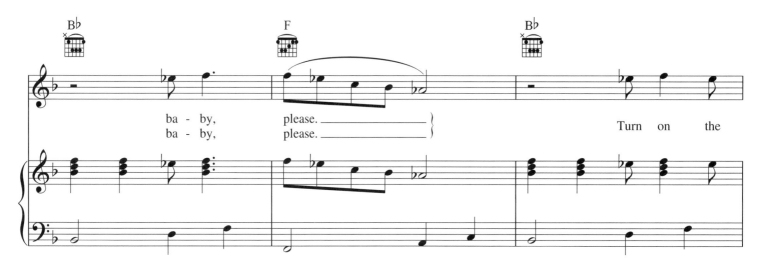

ba - by, please. _____
ba - by, please. _____ Turn on the

light, __ let it shine on me. _____

Turn on your love light, let it shine on me. __

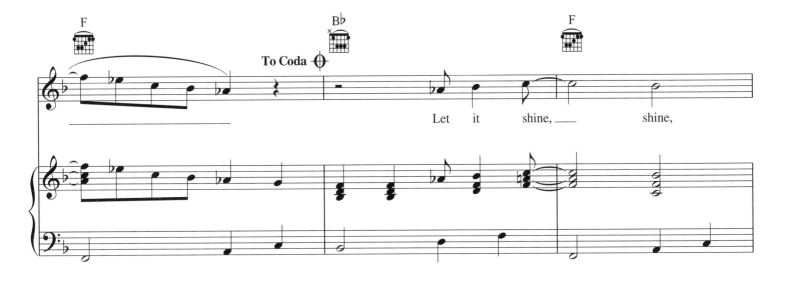

To Coda

Let it shine, __ shine,

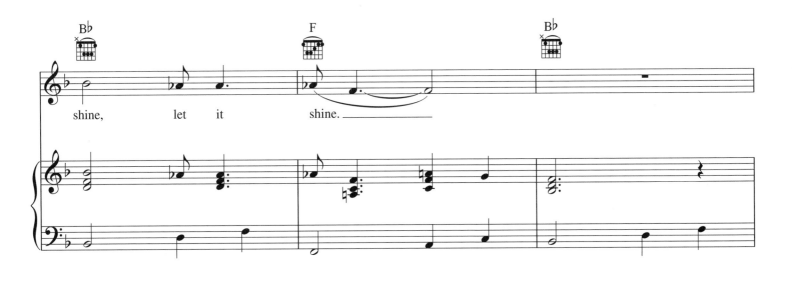

shine, let it shine. ___

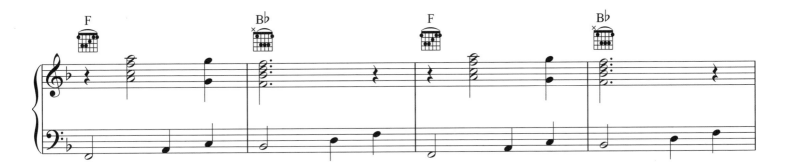

I get a lit - tle

A lit - tle bit high - er, a lit - tle bit

high - er, just a lit - tle bit high - er,

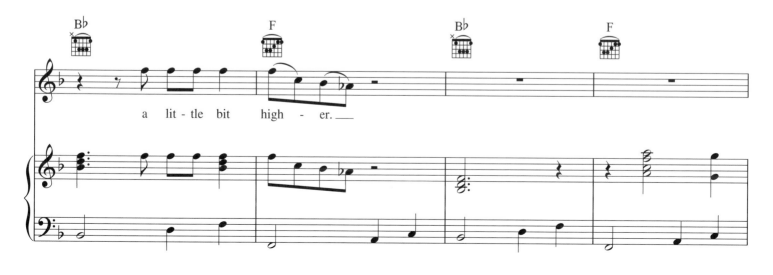

a lit - tle bit high - er. __

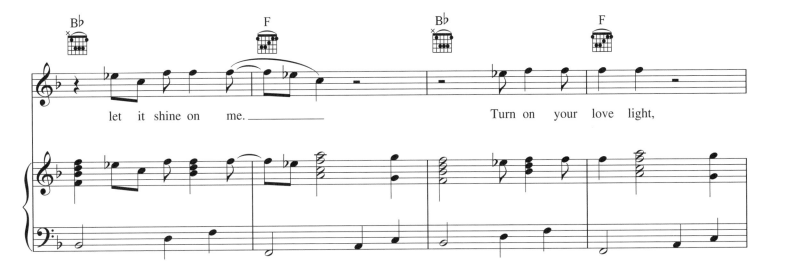

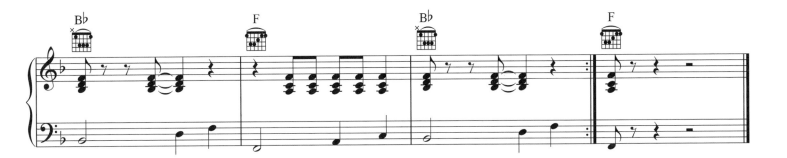

WE SHALL OVERCOME

Musical and Lyrical Adaptation by ZILPHIA HORTON,
FRANK HAMILTON, GUY CARAWAN and PETE SEEGER
Inspired by African American Gospel Singing, members of the Food and Tobacco
Workers Union, Charleston, SC, and the southern Civil Rights Movement

Moderately slow, with determination

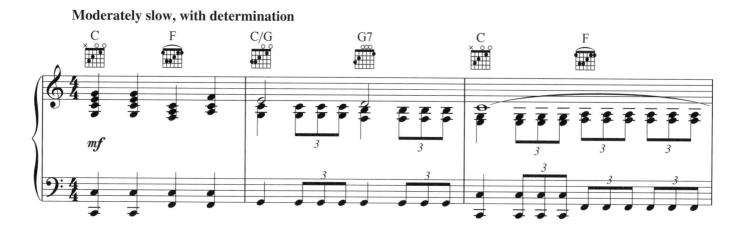

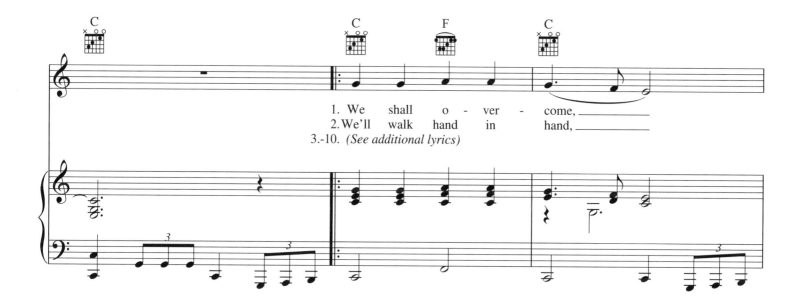

1. We shall o - ver - come, _____
2. We'll walk hand in hand, _____
3.-10. (See additional lyrics)

we shall o - ver - come, _____   we shall o - ver -
we'll walk hand in hand, _____   we'll walk hand in

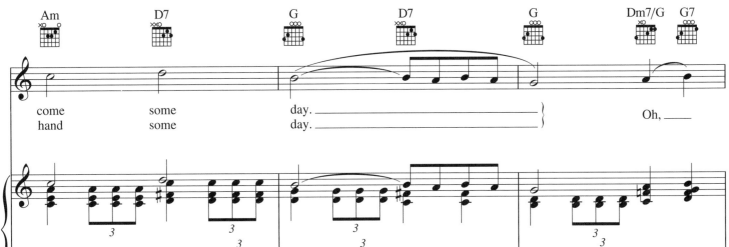

come   some   day.
hand   some   day.
     Oh, ___

deep   in   my   heart

I   do   be - lieve   we   shall   o - ver -

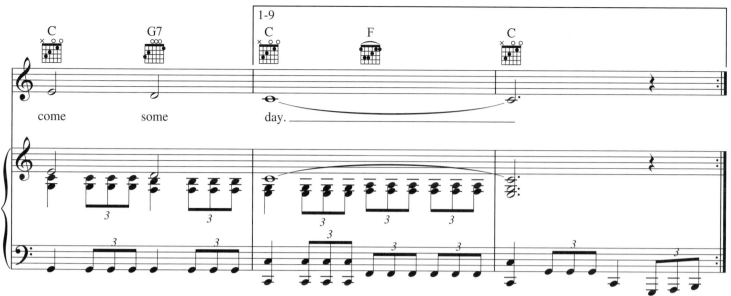

come   some   day.

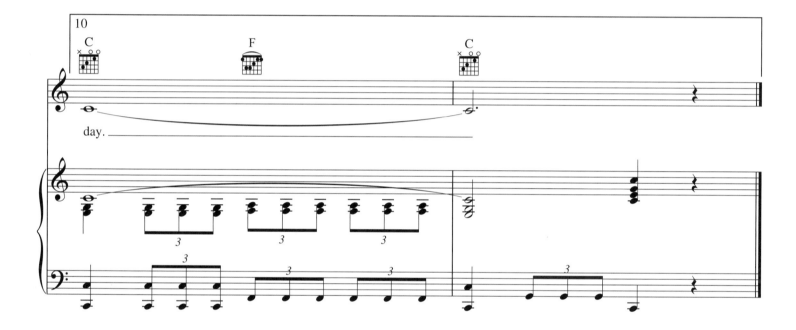

day.

Additional Lyrics

3. We are not afraid, we are not afraid,
   We are not afraid today.
   Oh, deep in my heart I do believe
   We shall overcome some day.

4. We shall stand together, we shall stand together,
   We shall stand together now.
   Oh, deep in my heart I do believe
   We shall overcome some day.

5. The truth will make us free, the truth will make us free,
   The truth will make us free some day.
   Oh, deep in my heart I do believe
   We shall overcome some day.

6. The Lord will see us through, the Lord will see us through,
   The Lord will see us through some day.
   Oh, deep in my heart I do believe
   We shall overcome some day.

7. We shall be like Him, we shall be like Him,
   We shall be like Him some day.
   Oh, deep in my heart I do believe
   We shall overcome some day.

8. We shall live in peace, we shall live in peace,
   We shall live in peace someday.
   Oh, deep in my heart I do believe
   We shall overcome some day.

9. The whole wide world around, the whole wide world around,
   The whole wide world around some day.
   Oh, deep in my heart I do believe
   We shall overcome some day.

10. We shall overcome, we shall overcome,
    We shall overcome some day.
    Oh, deep in my heart I do believe
    We shall overcome some day.

THE WEIGHT

By J.R. ROBERTSON

1. I pulled in-to Na-za-reth, was feel-in' 'bout half-past dead.
2.-5. *(See additional lyrics)*

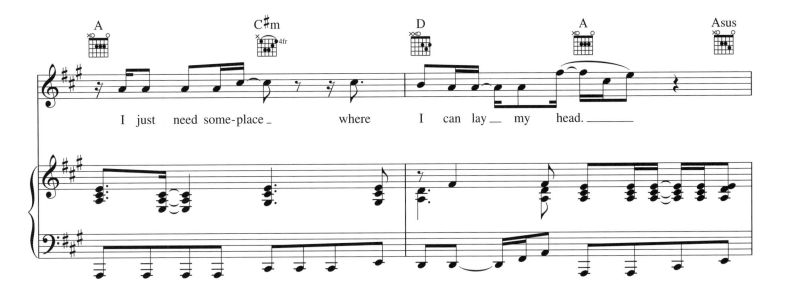

I just need some-place _ where I can lay _ my head. _____

Additional Lyrics

2. I picked up my bag, I went looking for a place to hide
   When I saw Carmen and the Devil walking side by side
   I said, "Hey, Carmen, come on, let's go down town."
   She said, "I gotta go but my friend can stick around."
   Chorus

3. Go down, Miss Moses, there's nothing you can say
   It's just ol' Luke and Luke's waiting on the judgement day
   "Well, Luke my friend, what about young Anna Lee?"
   He said, "Do me a favour, son, won't you stay
   and keep Anna Lee company?"
   Chorus

4. Crazy Chester followed me and he caught me in the fog
   He said, "I will fix your rack if you'll take Jack, my dog."
   I said, "Wait a minute Chester, you know a peaceful man."
   He said, "That's O.K. boy, won't you feed him when you can."
   Chorus

5. Catch a cannonball now, to take me down the line
   My bag is sinking low and I do believe it's time
   To get back to Miss Fanny, you know she's the only one
   Who sent me here with her regards for everyone.
   Chorus

WHITE RABBIT

Words and Music by
GRACE SLICK

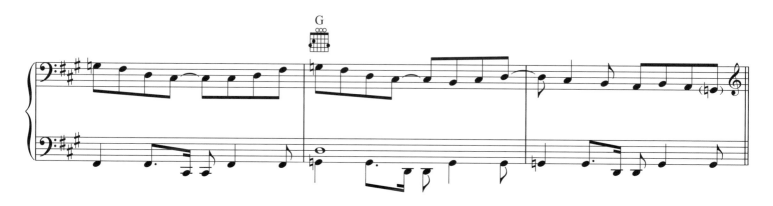

Psychedelic Stomp

chess - board _____ get up and tell you where to go. _____ and you've

just had some _ kind of mush - room, _____ and your mind is mov - ing low, _

_____ go ask Al - ice. _____ I think she'll know. _____

_____ When log - ic and pro - por - tion _____ have _ fall - en _____ slop - py

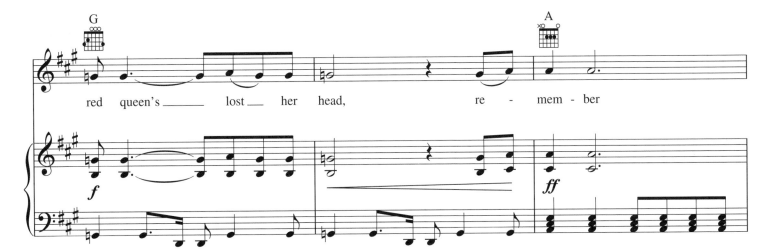

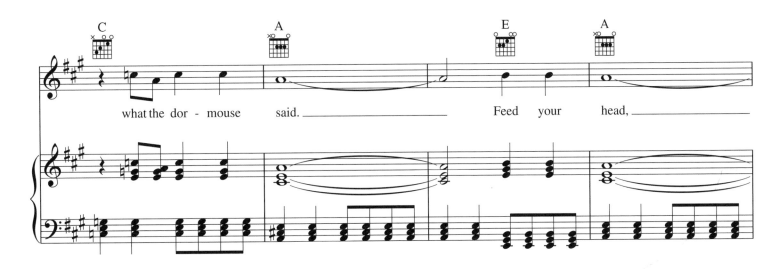

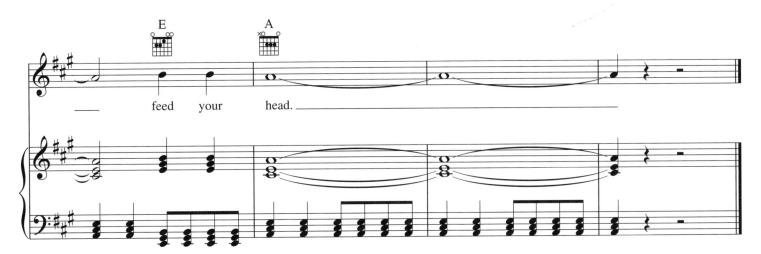

WITH A LITTLE HELP FROM MY FRIENDS

Words and Music by JOHN LENNON
and PAUL McCARTNEY

Slowly, in 2

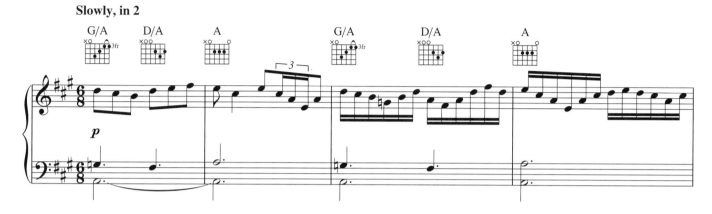

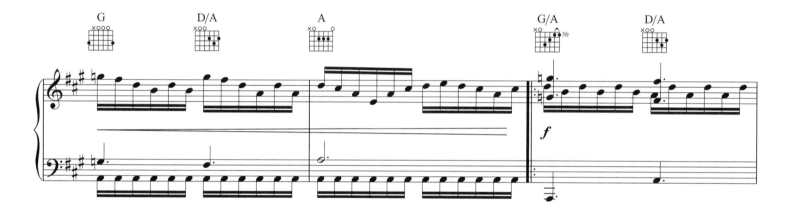

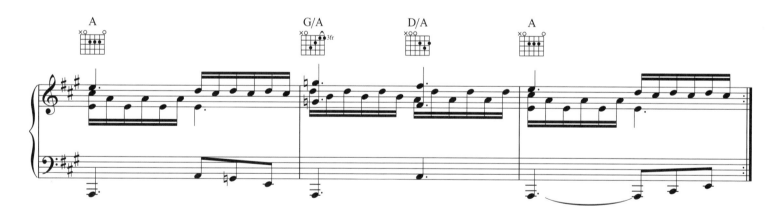

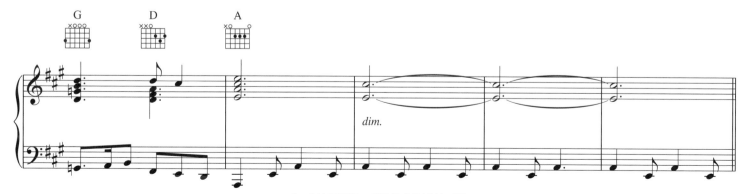

I said, I'm gon-na get ___ by... _____ with a lit-tle...
friends.   By   with a lit-tle help   from my

friends.   Woh, _____ yeah. _
                Woo,   woo,   woo.)

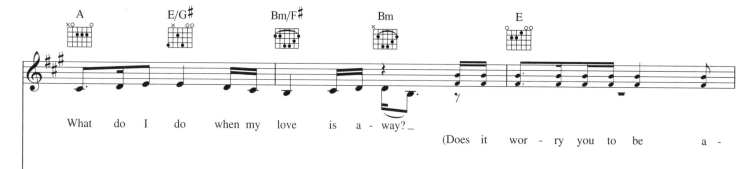

What do I do when my love is a-way? _
                                        (Does it wor-ry you to be a-

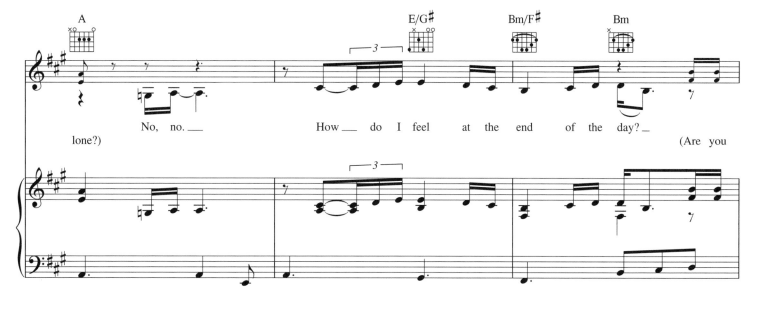

No, no.___ How___ do I feel at the end of the day?___ (Are you
lone?)

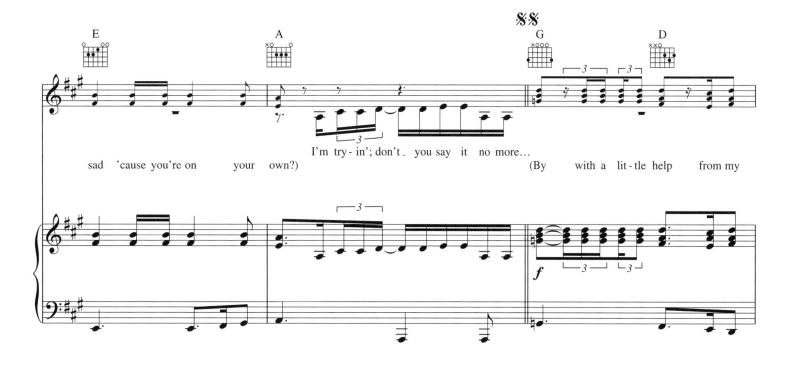

I'm try-in'; don't__ you say it no more...
sad 'cause you're on your own?) (By with a lit-tle help from my

*Gon - na get by with my friends,___ yeah.
friends. By with a lit-tle help from my

*2nd time, lead vocal ad lib

Lit - tle, lit - tle help. I'm gon - na try...

friends. By with a lit - tle help from my

Keep on help - ing out, oh, no.

friends. Woo, woo, woo.)

(Do you need an - y - bod - y?

*2nd time, lead vocal ad lib

WOODEN SHIPS

Words and Music by DAVID CROSBY,
STEPHEN STILLS and PAUL KANTNER

Moderately slow

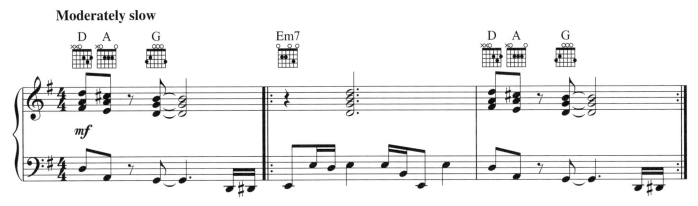

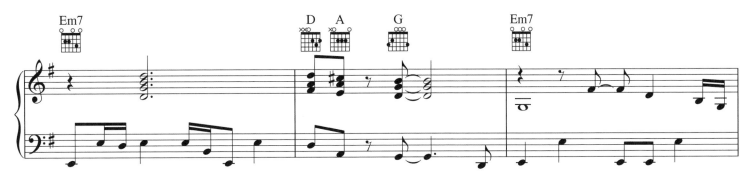

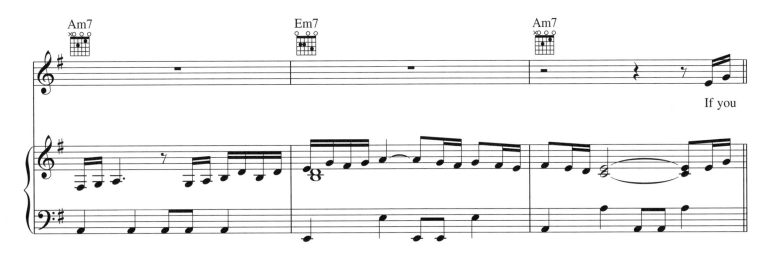

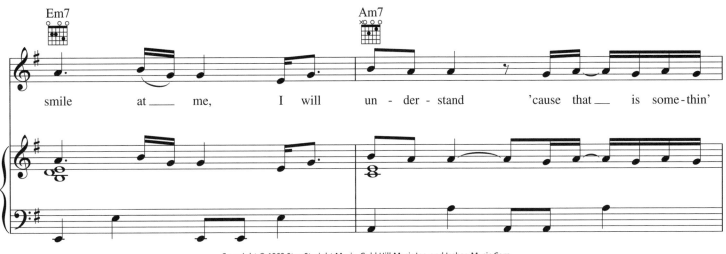

smile at ___ me, I will un - der - stand 'cause that ___ is some - thin'

If you

ev - 'ry-bod-y ev-'ry-where does in ___ the same ___

lan - guage. ___

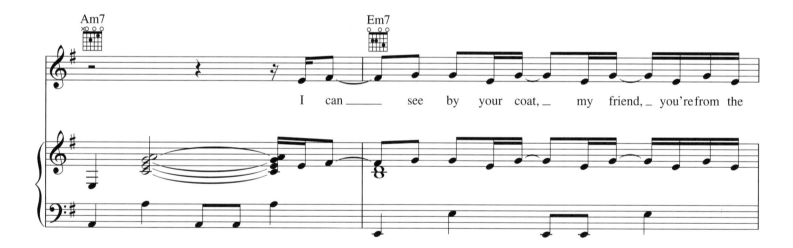

I can ___ see by your coat, ___ my friend, ___ you're from the

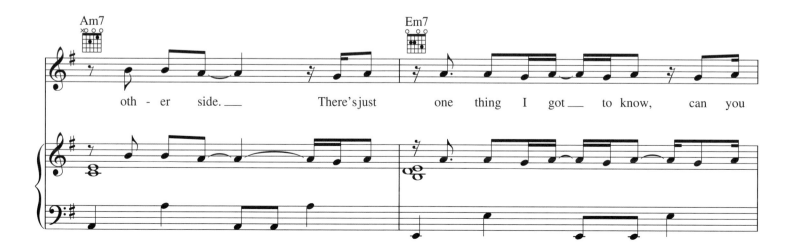

oth - er side. ___ There's just one thing I got ___ to know, can you

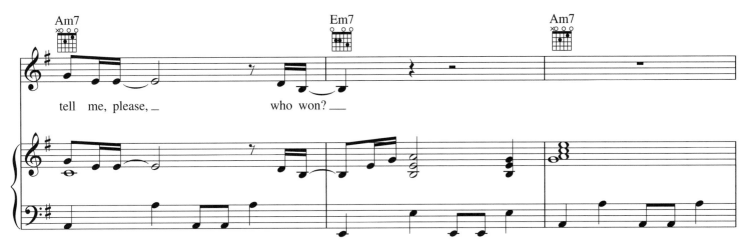

tell me, please, _____ who won? _____

Say, can I have some of your pur-ple ber-ries?

Yes, I've been eat-ing them _____ for six _____ or sev-en weeks now. Have-n't got

sick once. Prob-'ly keep _____ us both _____ a-live. _____

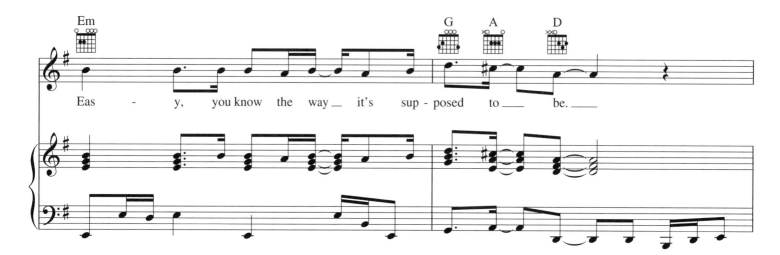

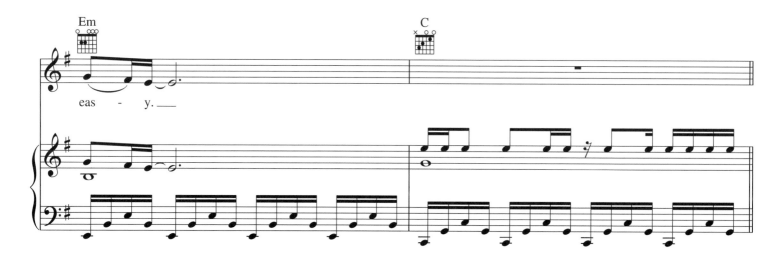

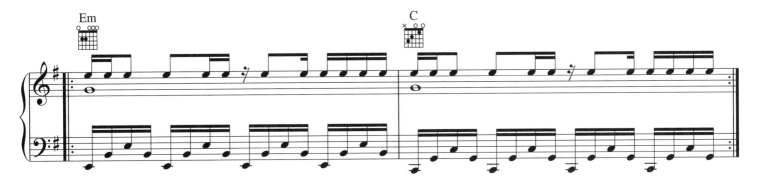

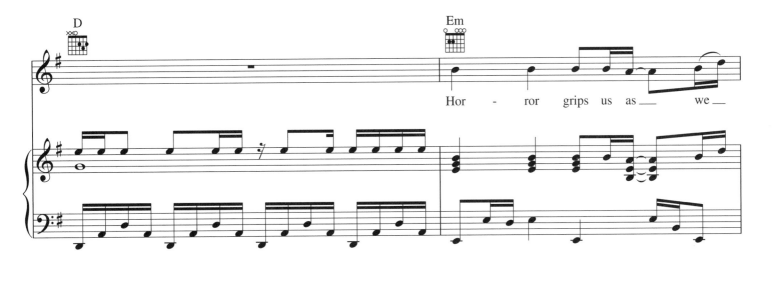

Hor - ror grips us as __ we __

watch you ___ die. ___ All we can do is ech - o your __

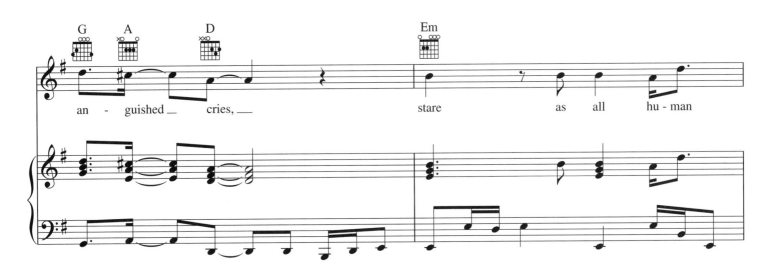

an - guished __ cries, ___ stare as all hu - man

feel - ings ___ die. ___ We are leav - ing, ___ you don't

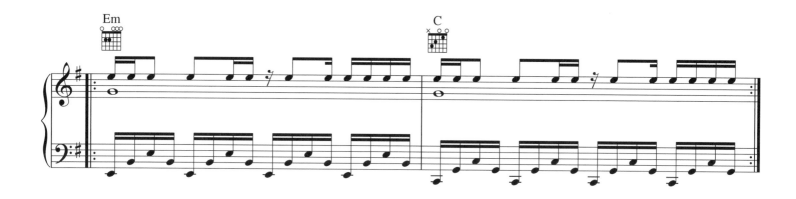

need ___ us.

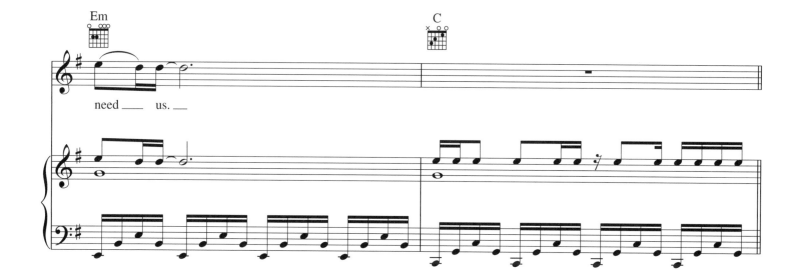

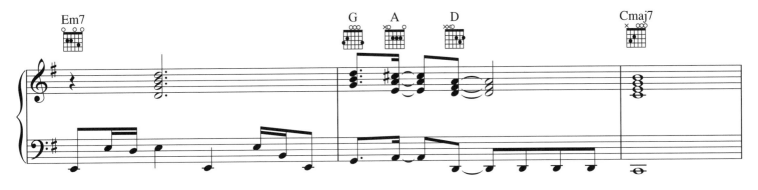

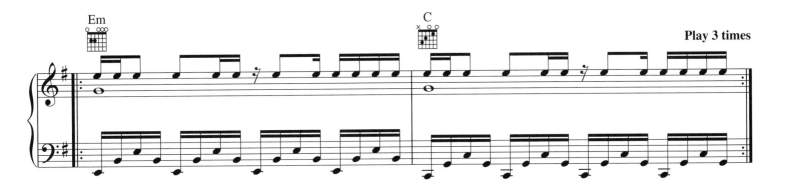

for - eign __ land, _____ far a - way, _____ where __ we might

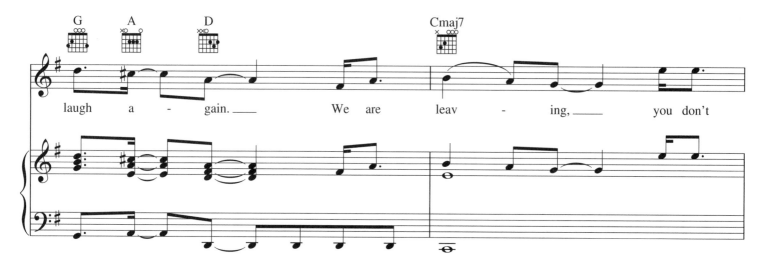

laugh a - gain. ___ We are leav - ing, ___ you don't

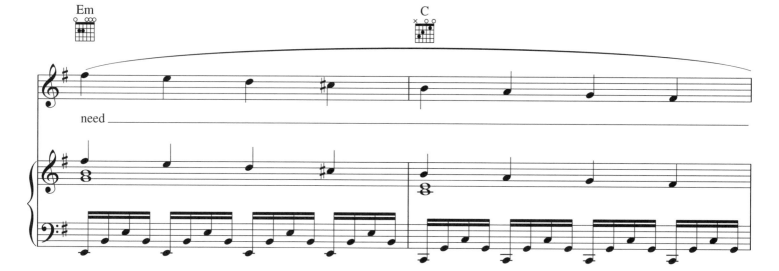

need _____

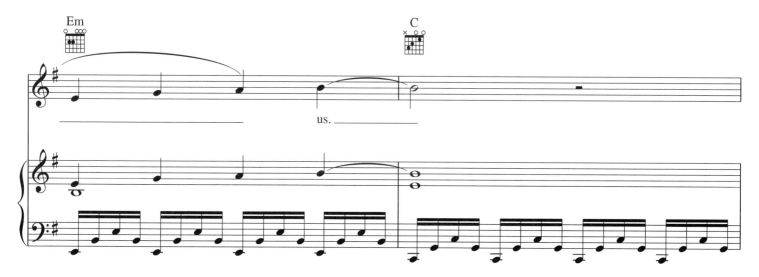

_____ us. _____

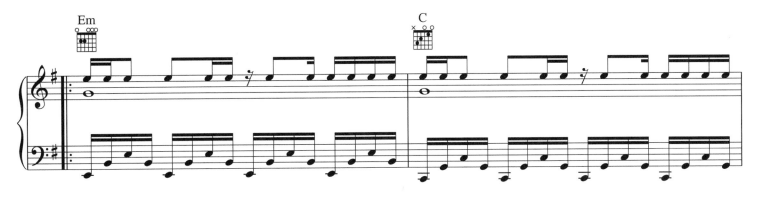

And it's a fair wind _ blow-in' warm out of the south o - ver my shoul - der. _

Guess I'll set a course and go. _

YOUNGER GENERATION

Words and Music by
JOHN SEBASTIAN

Moderately

Cmaj7

Why must ev-'ry gen-er-a - tion think __ their folks __ are square? __ And no mat-ter where their heads __ are, they know moms __ ain't there. __ 'Cause I

Dm

G7

Cmaj7

swore when I was small that I'd re - mem - ber when __

I knew what's wrong __ with them but I _____ was

small - er then. __

De - ter - mined to re - mem -
then I'll know that all __

- ber all _____ the card - 'nal rules, __ like
_____ I've learned _ my kid _____ as - sumes. _ And

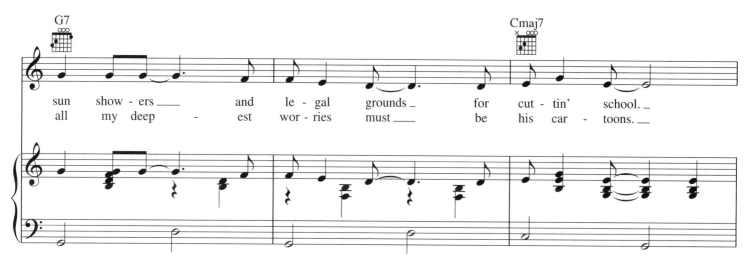

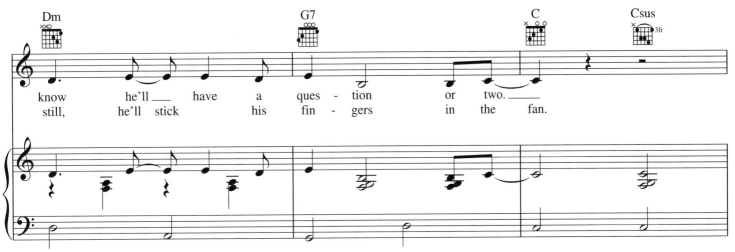

know   he'll ___ have   a   ques - tion   or   two. ___
still,   he'll stick   his   fin - gers   in   the   fan.

Like   "Hey,   Pop,   can   I ___
And   "Hey,   Pop,   my   girl -

___ go   ride ___ my   zoom? ___   It goes   two   hun - dred   miles ___
- friend's on - ly   three. ___   She's got her own   vid - e - o   phone ___

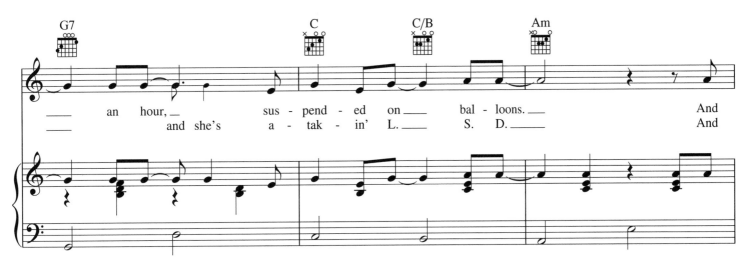

___ an   hour, ___   sus - pend - ed on ___ bal - loons. ___   And
___ and she's   a   tak - in'   L. ___   S.   D. ___   And

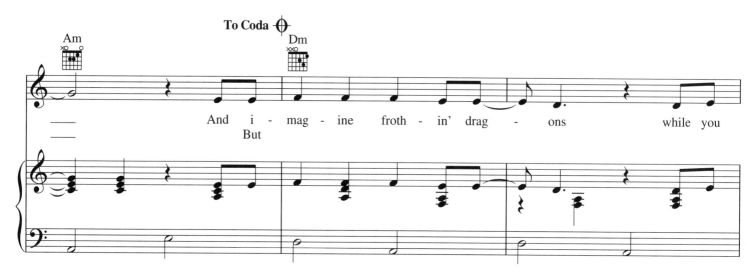

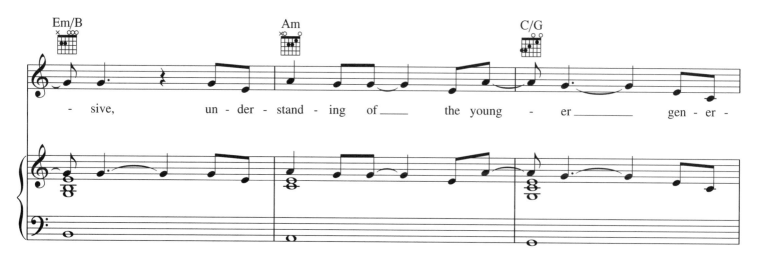

D.S. al Coda

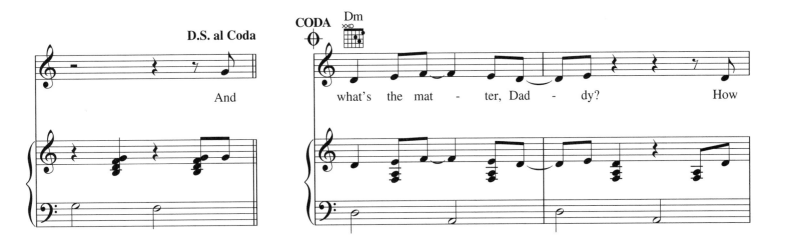

And what's the mat - ter, Dad - dy? How

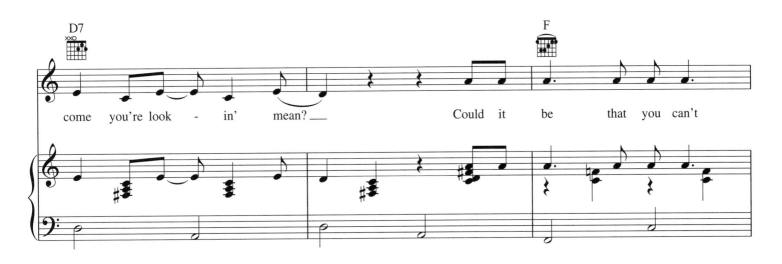

come you're look - in' mean? ___ Could it be that you can't

live up to your dreams?"